America's History through Young Voices

Using Primary Sources in the K–12 Social Studies Classroom

Richard M. Wyman, Jr.

California University of Pennsylvania

PEARSON

Boston ■ New York ■ San Francisco
Mexico City ■ Montreal ■ Toronto ■ London ■ Madrid ■ Munich ■ Paris
Hong Kong ■ Singapore ■ Tokyo ■ Cape Town ■ Sydney

Series Editor: *Traci Mueller*
Editorial Assistant: *Janice Hackenberg*
Senior Marketing Manager: *Krista Groshong*
Editorial-Production Service: *Omegatype Typography, Inc.*
Composition Buyer: *Linda Cox*
Manufacturing Buyer: *Andrew Turso*
Cover Administrator: *Joel Gendron*
Electronic Composition: *Omegatype Typography, Inc.*

For related titles and support materials, visit our online catalog
at www.ablongman.com.

Library of Congress Cataloging-in-Publication Data

Wyman, Richard M.
  America's history through young voices : using primary sources in the K–12
social studies classroom / Richard M. Wyman.
    p. cm.
  Includes bibiographical references.
  ISBN 0-205-39576-7 (alk. paper)
  1. United States—History—Study and teaching. 2. United States—History—
Sources. I. Title.

E175.8.W94 2004
973'.071'2—dc22

                                                                    2004054802

Printed in the United States of America

10 9 8   V036 15 14 13 12 11

*To Charlotte and Dick
for first instilling in me a love of history;*

*To Annie
for encouraging and supporting my love of history;*

*To Susan, Drew, Olivia, Hannah, and Eve
whom I hope will share my love of history.*

Contents

Preface

"I will keep a sort of journal of the time that may expire before I see thee: the perusal of it may some time hence give pleasure in a solitary hour to thee." Fourteen-year-old Sally Wister began her journal on September 25, 1777 expressing the hope that its contents might one day interest and amuse her closest friend, Deborah Norris. Little did Sally realize that over two hundred years later, historians would still read her journal to study the social customs and values of Colonial America through the eyes of a vivacious, articulate young woman.

Sally's journal is a primary source because she witnessed the events she described and wrote about them at the time those events occurred. A narrative such as Sally's journal "encourages readers to recognize the human aspects of history... and may help students maintain a balance between the abstractions of history as an intellectual exercise and history as an ongoing, participatory drama."[1] Sally's journal, however, also tells a story. It has a beginning, middle, and end, plus characters, setting, and a plot. It describes one individual's thoughts, emotions, and feelings at a particular point in time under a specific set of circumstances.

The goal of this book is to provide access to original accounts to enhance and improve instruction in social studies and history. With two exceptions, the primary sources in this book were all written by young people, aged thirteen to twenty-three. While the Slave Narratives from the Federal Writers' Project and the account by Ernest Green were written after the events described occurred, the authors related events from their youth. All the narratives therefore provide students with examples of U.S. history through the eyes of individuals close to their own age.

The history presented here is of ordinary people, not that of empire-builders, kings, and presidents. The diaries of Sally Wister and David How depict two different points of view of the American Revolution. In letters to her father, Mary Paul describes life as a mill girl during the early stages of the American industrial revolution. The diaries of Sallie Hester and Swen

---

[1]Levstik, L. S., & Barton, K. C. (2001). *Doing history: Investigating with children in elementary and middle schools* (2nd ed., p. 120). Mahwah, NJ: Lawrence Erlbaum Associates.

Swensson describe two epic migrations: the pioneer crossing on the Overland Trail and the immigrant journey to America. Life during periods of war are portrayed from three very different perspectives: the diary of C. W. Hadley, a young Union soldier from Iowa fighting in the Civil War; letters from junior high school students to Sergeant Armstrong, a former history teacher fighting in France during World War I; and letters from Mary Anna Martin, World War II WASP (Women Airforce Service Pilot). The despair and suffering caused by the Great Depression are revealed through the poignant letters written by young Americans to First Lady Eleanor Roosevelt. The Civil Rights Movement is described through the voice of Ernest Green, the first African American graduate of Central High School in Little Rock, Arkansas. Finally, two disgraceful periods of U.S. history are exposed through the reminiscent accounts of former slaves and the essays of interned Japanese Americans during World War II.

The primary sources are drawn from the historical periods covered in a standard social studies/U.S. history curriculum, and thus can be used to supplement and enhance the content of a traditional textbook. The great value of primary sources, however, lies in the opportunities that they provide for interpretation, analysis, and critical thinking. These are skills historians use when they "do" history.

Chapter 1 presents a general introduction to historical sources; primary and secondary sources are defined and described, and different categories of primary sources are listed along with examples of each type. Skill development through the use of primary sources is described in depth. Connections are made between the use of primary sources and standards at both the national and state levels. At the end of the chapter, general classroom activities are presented, which can be used with a wide variety of primary sources.

The diaries, letters, essays, and reminiscences begin in Chapter 2. A brief introduction preceding each narrative is intended to place the primary source into a historical context, identify the major topics, and provide background information on the author or authors. Specific instructional activities organized around five categories of historical thinking skills conclude each chapter.

Some of the narratives, especially the diaries, were shortened due to length considerations. What was omitted was obviously my decision, and I made every effort to maintain the integrity, accuracy, and readability of the original account. The primary sources otherwise appear in their original form. This means that spelling errors, grammatical mistakes, awkward sentences, and so on appear exactly as the author wrote them.

The young people whose voices are heard through the primary sources selected for this book reveal common and consistent human traits that people of all eras share: hope, despair, happiness, sorrow, pride, humility, prejudice, tolerance, courage, fear, love, and hate. Their accounts can help young people of today "locate their individual lives in the chain of generations . . . find common bonds with people far off in time and space, recognizing in them our common humanity, while understanding the differences that may separate us" and "develop a sense of perspective that makes their world of today more understandable."[2]

Acknowledgments

David McCullough, in an interview discussing his work as a writer and historian, remarked that, "I couldn't do what I do without librarians . . . I can't tell you how many times I've had problems worked out or discoveries made possible by librarians who've taken an interest in what I'm doing."[3] I am indebted to the following librarians who took an interest in my work and introduced me to the young people whose words and voices appear in this book: Russ Taylor, Harold B. Lee Library, Brigham Young University; David Smolen, New Hampshire Historical Society; Suzanne Crowe and Glenn L. McMullen, Indiana Historical Society; Anne Prichard, Special Collections, University of Arkansas Libraries; Paul A. Carnahan, Vermont Historical Society; and Tracey MacGowen, Blagg-Huey Library, Texas Woman's University.

Because I am a professional educator but an amateur historian, writing the chapter introductions required reading many journal articles and books. These materials were acquired through the skilled assistance of Diane Turosik, Interlibrary Loan Technician, and Barbara Sabo, Circulation Coordinator, of the Louis L. Manderino Library at California University of Pennsylvania.

Preliminary research and writing for this book were done during a sabbatical leave in the fall of 2002. For that wonderful opportunity, I am indebted to Dr. Audrey-Beth Fitch and my other colleagues on the University-Wide Sabbatical Committee. I also wish to thank Dr. Angelo Armenti, Jr., President; Dr. Curtis Smith, Academic Vice-President; and Ms. Geraldine Jones, Dean of the College of Education and Human Services at California University of Pennsylvania for their support of my sabbatical leave.

I would also like to thank the reviewers of this edition: Vaughn Dailey, Peters Township Middle School; Keith Emmerling, Thomas Jefferson High

[2]Meltzer, M. (1993). Voices from the past. In M. O. Tunnell & R. Ammon (Eds.) *The story of ourselves: Teaching history through children's literature* (p. 29). Portsmouth, NH: Heinemann.

[3]Shaver, L. (April 2003). The storyteller: An interview with David McCullough (p. 40). *Information Outlook, 7*, 4.

School; Mary E. Haas, West Virginia University; Margaret A. Laughlin, University of Wisconsin; Janet Strickland, State University of W. Georgia; and Barry L. Witten, Western Illinois University.

Finally, greatest thanks go to my wife, Dr. Andrea Wyman, a gifted writer and a skilled editor. For more than two years, she patiently and enthusiastically listened, advised, and encouraged. The coherent thoughts and ideas in this book are primarily due to her skill. I take full responsibility for all the others.

1

Historical Sources

Primary sources have the capacity to make history come alive by adding an exciting and valuable dimension to social studies and history. Diaries, letters, essays, and reminiscences open a window into the past by returning "readers to the face-to-face world of everyday life . . . as people experienced it then."[1] Look through that window now and you'll see a young woman in 1849 about to begin a long and dangerous journey.

Primary Sources

St. Joseph, Missouri was a bustling place in 1849 when Sallie Hester and her family began their journey to California on the Overland Trail. Sallie wrote in her diary "As far as the eye can reach, so great is the emigration, you see nothing but wagons. This town presents a striking appearance—a vast army on wheels—crowds of men, women and lots of children and last but not least the cattle and horses upon which our lives depend." Sallie's diary is a primary source and can be studied by historians to learn what life was like during the great American migration west.

Eyewitness and Timing Rules

A primary source is evidence created by individuals or peoples who *witnessed* or participated in an event at the time the event occurred. Sallie's diary is an excellent example of a primary source because it contains descriptions of events to which she was an eyewitness: thousands of men, women, and children preparing for the long road west in St. Joseph, Missouri. The diaries, letters,

---

[1]Meltzer, M. (1993). Voices from the past. In M. O. Tunnell & Ammon, R. (Ed.) *The story of ourselves: Teaching history through children's literature*. Portsmouth, NH: Heinemann (p. 29).

essays, and reminiscences selected for this book meet this definition: they were written by individuals who actually witnessed the events described.

A somewhat more exacting definition of primary source includes a second factor: the *time* at which the document was created. Why would historians value working with eyewitness accounts written at the time the events described occurred? The reason is simple: the less time that elapses between the events and their description, the more likely the account is valid and reliable. One can imagine Sallie sitting down by the campfire the night after arriving in St. Joseph and recording her thoughts about what she observed that day. She was a witness to the events described in her diary and she wrote about them at the time they occurred. The sights, sounds, and smells were all fresh in her mind, thus providing the historian with a rich, detailed, and likely accurate account of St. Joseph at the height of the migration west. Sallie's diary and the other primary sources in this book, with two exceptions, satisfy the most exacting definition of a primary source: first, it was recorded by an eyewitness, and second, it was written at the time the events described occurred.

Reminiscent Accounts

Reminiscent accounts, or memoirs, are descriptions of historical events written after the events occurred. A good example of this is that most emigrants making the overland trip west did not keep diaries. Perhaps urged by a relative or an acquaintance, however, they chose to write about their experiences long after the journey ended. These documents are considered primary sources although they adhere to only the eyewitness rule. Authors of reminiscences were clearly witness to or participants in the events described, but the events are documented long after they occurred. Notes, correspondence, interviews, and the author's memory are used to recall and write about the actual events.

The Slave Narratives from the Federal Writers' Project (Chapter 7) and the narrative by Ernest Green (Chapter 13) are the lone reminiscent accounts in this book. Only a very small percentage of slaves knew how to read and write and as the slave narratives make clear, the punishment for those who had the skills and used them was severe. Accounts by slaves written during the period of their enslavement are almost nonexistent. Therefore, historians interested in studying slavery through the eyes of those who experienced it must rely almost exclusively on reminiscent accounts.

Why do historians use reminiscent accounts? For some periods or events in American history, these are the only accounts available. In other cases, such as the Ernest Green narrative, the reminiscent account provides information and insight into an event difficult to find in other primary sources. Regardless of the reason, what is critical to the historian or student of history is that a reminiscent account be identified as such. The content can then be interpreted and analyzed with the clear understanding that time and personal motives often distort memories.

Accuracy and Reliability of Primary Sources

Many people read a diary, letter, or essay and assume it presents an accurate picture of the events described. Students frequently make this mistake because they "do not necessarily approach narratives with a critical eye: if they encounter information in the form of a story, they may assume that it is true simply because they are so caught up in the story itself."[2] Students could easily construe the content of the narratives in this book as accurate and reliable. However, a significant component of historical research involves learning to judge the accuracy and reliability of sources. This is a key skill to learn. The questions contained in Figure 1.1 are adapted from a worksheet created by the Library of Congress, and are ones historians ask as they attempt to judge the reliability and quality of historical narratives. When students respond to the questions in Figure 1.1, they are interpreting, analyzing, and evaluating a historical narrative. They are 'doing' the work of historians.

Skilled historians know that "using multiple sources can lead to a fuller picture of the past than relying on any single source—one of the most basic principles of historical research."[3] No historical account, including the primary sources in this book, is totally objective. There are thousands of diaries chronicling the Overland Trail experience, some even containing descriptions of the same event or location. But because writers filter what they say through their experiences and biases, explanations and descriptions of the same event

---

FIGURE 1.1   *Judging Reliability and Quality*

---

1. Who created the source and why?
2. Was it created through a spur-of-the-moment act, a routine transaction, or a thoughtful process?
3. Did the author have first-hand knowledge of the event? Or did the author report what others saw and heard?
4. Was the author a neutral party, or did the creator have opinions or interests that might have influenced what was recorded?
5. Did the author produce the source for personal use, for one or more individuals, or for a large audience?
6. Did the author wish to inform or persuade others?
7. Did the author have reasons to be honest or dishonest?
8. Was the information recorded during the event, immediately after the event, or after some lapse of time?
9. Can the information in the narrative be corroborated by another source?

---

[2]Barton, K. C. (1997). History—It can be elementary (p. 15). *Social Education, 6*(11).

[3]Levstik, L. S., & Barton, K. (2001). *Doing history: Investigating with children in elementary and middle schools* (2nd ed., p. 32). Mahwah, NJ: Lawrence Erlbaum Associates.

can vary dramatically. Each narrative in this book is one person's account of the events described. Sallie Hester's diary represents *Sallie's* account of her experiences on the Overland Trail. She made conscious decisions regarding both what to include and omit and the words used to describe her observations are hers alone.

It is also important to remember that no accomplished historian studying the Overland Trail experience or any other period of U.S. history would rely on a single primary source. Although the content of the narrative may be historically accurate, it still is one individual's perspective. When studying one of the historical periods covered in this book, seek out additional primary and secondary sources for information.

To the best of my knowledge, the primary sources in this book were all written at the time the events described occurred, with the exceptions being the Slave Narratives from the Federal Writers' Project and the account by Ernest Green. That does not, however, necessarily mean that all the narratives are in the same form as originally written by the authors. This is especially true with the diaries, because the great majority were not written for public viewing. Individuals wrote diaries for personal reasons, as a creative outlet, to keep a record of important personal or family events, or to pass some family history on to descendents.

It is also entirely possible that at some point during a diary's history, editing occurred. A family member, an overzealous publisher, or a schoolteacher neighbor of the diarist's granddaughter may have altered what was originally written. Even the original author may have gone back and changed entries. Revisions may be insignificant, such as correcting spelling and grammatical errors, or they could be far more serious, such as significantly altering the content of the diary or eliminating passages entirely. In order to accurately interpret the narrative, historians often acknowledge the fact that the diaries may not appear as they were originally written. What helps is when other sources are consulted and facts and observations are cross-checked for accuracy and reliability.

Types of Primary Sources

Many primary sources used in the study of history are, like the ones in this book, written documents. However, the universe of primary sources is far more varied than the written or printed word. Primary sources can be divided into six categories and these, along with examples of each type, are listed in Figure 1.2. Although the list is not all-inclusive, it shows the diversity of primary sources available to the historian, classroom teacher, and student in their study of the past. All of the artifacts listed in Figure 1.2 are valuable sources for historical analysis and interpretation and can be used with narratives to expand knowledge and understanding of a particular event or period in U.S. history. Consulting historic maps of the Oregon Trail, analyzing yearly census

FIGURE 1.2   *Categories of Primary Sources*

Categories of Primary Sources	Examples
Written Documents	Letters, diaries, manuscripts
Government Documents	Census records, government reports, official correspondence, birth certificates
Printed Documents	Books, magazine articles, newspaper articles
Visual Artifacts	Photographs, films, illustrations, maps, cartoons, posters, paintings, drawings
Oral Artifacts	Oral histories, recorded speeches, music
Physical Artifacts	Furniture, tools, appliances, toys, clothing

records of California and Oregon, and examining emigrant guidebooks are three examples of activities that can be used along with Sallie Hester's diary in studying westward expansion.

Archival photographs are perhaps the most widely accessible and versatile of the different types of primary sources listed in Figure 1.2 and they are excellent data sources for interpretation and analysis. Although the photograph of Devil's Gate in Figure 1.3 was taken a little more than twenty years after Sallie's trip, its physical features and those of the surrounding landscape are probably very similar to what Sallie encountered on July 2 in 1849. She wrote in her diary: "We made our way to the very edge of the cliff and looked down. We could hear the water dashing, splashing and roaring as if angry at the small space through which it was forced to pass." Using the photograph, Sallie's diary, and other sources, students can:

- describe what they see in the photograph.
- hypothesize as to its location.
- hypothesize as to why it was named "Devil's Gate."
- locate Devil's Gate on a map.
- determine the climate of the region.
- write a narrative describing an imaginary climb up Devil's Gate.

Photographs and other types of visual artifacts add an exciting dimension to the study of any historical period. Hundreds of thousands of photographs, paintings, drawings, posters, maps, and cartoons are now accessible online through the Prints and Photographs (P&P) Online Catalog of the Library of Congress (http://lcweb.loc.gov/rr/print/catalog.html) and the National Archives and Records Administration (www.archives.gov/index.html).

FIGURE 1.3 Looking west from over Devil's Gate showing the plains of the Sweetwater, the Oregon Trail, and the Seminole Mountains in the distance. (ARC Identifier 516897, Variant Control Number NWDNS-57-HS-288, National Archives and Records Administration, College Park, MD)

Secondary Sources

Let's say that an author of a history textbook wanted to write a segment on westward expansion; consulting a primary source such as Sallie Hester's diary would likely be the first step. While the author's description of St. Joseph may be very similar to that of Sallie's, the passage written by the historian is a secondary source because it is someone else's interpretation or analysis of an event. The passage was also not written at the time the events occurred, nor was the historian an eyewitness to those events.

Secondary sources are an excellent means to gain an overall understanding of an event or historical period and consulting them does not constitute a criminal act. The true value of secondary sources, however, is that they can be used to cross-check the accuracy and reliability of primary sources. The study of any period in U.S. history should invariably include the use of secondary sources such as a history or social studies textbook.

National Standards for History

Curriculum standards denote the outcomes of instruction. They provide direction as to the content and skills that should be taught and are used by policy makers, curriculum specialists, administrators, and teachers as instructional guides. Standards recognize the importance of primary sources in the teaching of social studies and history and have been developed at both the national and state levels.

The *National Standards for History,* published by the National Center for History in the Schools in 1996, identified two major categories of standards: historical understandings and historical thinking skills. Historical understandings "define what students should know about the history of families, their communities, states, nation, and world."[4] Historical understandings encompass the content or knowledge of what should be taught in social studies and history.

Historical thinking skills, on the other hand, "enable children to differentiate past, present, and future time; raise questions; seek and evaluate evidence; compare and analyze historical stories, illustrations, and records from the past; interpret the historical record; and construct historical narratives of their own."[5] Historical thinking skills describe what students should be doing with and to the content (historical understandings). The five categories of historical thinking skills are presented and described in Figure 1.4.[6]

Historical understandings are taught in every social studies classroom. These are the names, dates, places, and other facts that all of us remember (or more likely forgot) from our social studies experience. Educated citizens, however, possess both knowledge and skills, for it is the latter that prepare them "to detect bias, to weigh evidence, and to evaluate judgments . . . to make sensible, independent judgments, to sniff out spurious appeals to history by partisan pleaders, to distinguish between anecdote and analysis."[7] Successful development of these skills cannot be accomplished if the sole source of content in social studies or history is the textbook. To learn and apply many of the historical thinking skills described in Figure 1.4, students must have access to multiple sources of content. Primary sources allow for both the teaching of content and the skills essential to effective citizenship contained in state and national standards for history and social studies.

None of the five categories of historical thinking skills can be taught or learned in isolation, either from each other or from some kind of content. All

[4]National Center for History in the Schools. (1996). *National standards for history* (p. 2). Los Angeles, CA: Author.

[5]Ibid., p. 2.

[6]Ibid., pp. 6–7.

[7]Ibid, p. 49.

FIGURE 1.4   *Types of Historical Thinking*

Chronological thinking. Developing a beginning sense of historical time—past, present, and future—in order to identify the temporal sequence in which events occurred, measure calendar time, interpret and create time lines, and explain patterns of historical continuity and change.

Historical comprehension. Includes the ability to listen to and read historical stories and narratives with understanding; to identify the basic elements of the narrative or story structure (the characters, situation, sequence of events, their causes, and their outcome); and to develop the ability to describe the past through the eyes and experiences of those who were there, as revealed through their literature, art, artifacts, and other records of their time.

Historical analysis and interpretation. Includes the ability to compare and contrast different experiences, beliefs, motives, traditions, hopes, and fears of people from various groups and backgrounds, and at various times in the past and present; to analyze how these differing motives, interests, beliefs, hopes, and fears influenced people's behaviors; to compare the different perspectives included in different stories about historical people and events; to compare historical fiction and documentary sources about a particular era or event; and to analyze the historical accuracy of fictional accounts.

Historical research capabilities. Includes the ability to formulate historical questions from encounters with historical documents, artifacts, photos, visits to historical sites, and eyewitness accounts; to acquire information concerning the historical time and place where the artifact, document, or other record was created; and to construct a historical narrative or story concerning it.

Historical issues-analysis and decision-making. Includes the ability to identify problems that people confronted in historical literature, the local community, and the state; to analyze the various interests and points of view of people caught up in these situations; to evaluate alternative proposals for dealing with the problem; and to analyze whether the decisions reached or the actions taken were good ones and why.

five should be incorporated into instruction when using primary sources. Activities designed to foster the development of these skills are presented at the end of each chapter.

Another well-known set of national standards for social studies was developed by the National Council for the Social Studies (NCSS), the professional organization for social studies teachers at all educational levels. Ten thematic strands constitute the knowledge and skills essential in social studies instruction. Diaries, letters, and essays are sources of content that can be used to address the goals outlined in the NCSS standards.

State Standards

Teachers are held accountable not for national standards, but for the standards that exist at the state level. State standards are usually available on the website of every state department of education, and the value and importance of incorporating primary sources into the curriculum are well recognized at the state level.

Many states have drawn from the work of the National Center for History in the Schools (www.sscnet.ucla.edu/nchs) to develop their own standards for social studies and history education. In the state of California, to cite one example, "the use of biographies, original documents, diaries, letters, legends, speeches, and other narrative artifacts from our past is encouraged to foster students' understanding of historical events by revealing the ideas, values, fears, and dreams of the people associated with them."[8] State social studies and history standards often provide support for the inclusion of primary sources in the curriculum.

Primary Sources in the Classroom

To increase the likelihood that the narratives in this book will be enjoyed and effectively used, preliminary activities can be conducted to introduce students to primary sources, what they are, and how to use them when conducting historical research. The Library of Congress and the National Archives and Records Administration are the two largest repositories of primary sources in this country, and each has developed excellent lessons to introduce students to these types of historical sources.

The Learning Page of Library of Congress (http://memory.loc.gov/ammem/ndlpedu/lessons/psources/source.html) has a lesson entitled 'What Are Primary Sources,' in which students are asked the question, "What kind of historical records do you leave behind in your daily life?" Students record activities that they were involved in and then attempt to identify evidence of these activities that was left behind.

The Digital Classroom of the National Archives and Records Administration contains an introductory activity (www.archives.gov/digital_classroom/introductory_activity.html), which involves students in collecting and analyzing personal documents such as birth certificates, photographs, and report cards. Both lesson plans introduce the concept of primary sources by linking the topic to events and documents from the students' own lives. Students learn they are both creating and using primary sources every day.

---

[8]California State Board of Education, *Introduction, History-Social Science Content Standards* (www.cde.ca.gov/standards/history/intro.html).

Using Diaries, Letters, and Essays

The goal of this book is to make available to teachers and students first-hand accounts from twelve periods of American history that will complement and enhance a traditional curriculum and textbook. The narratives can be used as the principal source of content for your students, but additional primary and secondary sources will be required.

The value of using primary sources lies in the opportunities these documents provide for analysis, interpretation, assessment, and critical thinking. These are the same skills historians use when conducting historical research, and are nearly impossible to develop and foster in students when the sole source of content is the textbook.

Instructional activities are included at the end of each chapter and are organized around the five categories of historical thinking skills. Each set of activities is specific to the primary source contained in that chapter, although some will necessitate access to additional resources. There are, however, general techniques and activities that can be done with a majority, if not all, of the diaries, letters, and essays in this book. These activities, as well, require students to use one or more of the historical thinking skills. Rather than repeat these activities and techniques at the end of every chapter, the eight are briefly described and explained below.

Judging Accuracy and Reliability.   Assess the accuracy and reliability of the primary source by responding to the nine questions contained in Figure 1.1.

Translate.   Paraphrase parts of a diary, letter, or essay. Rephrasing portions of the primary source requires comprehension and interpretation.

Unexpected Events.   Read the primary source and note any incidents or events that are unexpected, interesting, or confusing. The results will provide topics that hold special interest to students, which is valuable information when planning instruction.

Recurring Events.   List subjects and events that appear on a recurring basis in the primary source. These topics reveal what was critical to the success of the endeavor as well as what was of interest to the individual author.

Language.   Ascertain the meaning of peculiar vocabulary contained in the primary sources. Sally Wister's journal and the diary of David How, in particular, possess language distinctive to the historical time period.

Imaginary Diary or Letters.   Write imaginary diary entries or letters using the same format and structure found in the originals. To make the content of the imaginary diary or letters historically accurate, some knowledge of the time period is essential.

Textbook Analysis. Compare the content of the primary source with how the same historical time period is described in the textbook, noting and discussing similarities and differences. Students will also likely discover that primary sources contain far more detail and information about a particular historical period than does a textbook, thus raising the question, "Why was certain content included in the textbook and other content omitted?"

Trade Book Analysis. Compare the depiction of the period and events in the primary source with that of a trade book on the same subject. Outstanding historical fiction, nonfiction, and biographies have been written about the same historical time periods represented by the primary sources.

Organization of This Book

Each chapter begins with a short introduction designed to place the primary source into an historical context, identify the major topics, and provide biographical information, where available, on the author or authors. Following the primary source, the "In the Classroom" section contains instructional activities organized around the five categories of historical thinking skills.

2

Colonial America: The Journal of Sally Wister

When sixteen-year-old Sally Wister could no longer write to or receive letters from her best friend, Deborah Norris, she began a journal. "Tho' I have not the least shadow of an opportunity to send a letter, if I do write, I will keep a sort of journal of the time that may expire before I see thee." Sally and her family had left their Market Street home in Philadelphia for the safety of her aunt's farm fifteen miles from the city when the British captured New York in late 1776. Nearly a year later, military activity around Philadelphia and the impending occupation of the colonial capital by British troops made it impossible for Sally and Deborah, still residing in the city, to continue their correspondence by letter.

Sally wrote the journal to share her experiences, emotions, and thoughts with a trusted confidante. Thus we are treated to a sincere and vivid picture of a bright, charming, and flirtatious young woman living during the early years of the American Revolution. Through her words, we learn something of the manners, customs, and values of a young colonial girl, and also of the significant historical events to which Sally was a witness and participant.

The Wisters were members of the Religious Society of Friends, or Quakers, a religious group that values plain and simple living. Her family's wealth, however, made possible the elegant clothes that Sally speaks of admiringly and frequently in her journal. "[W]ent up to dress, put on a new purple and white striped Persian, white petticoat, muslin apron, gauze cap, and handkerchief."

Due to her family's financial and social status, Sally was educated at an exclusive school for girls in Philadelphia. This, however, was an opportunity denied to most other young women. At school, she was taught the traditional subjects such as literature and arithmetic as well as some French and Latin. At the time, young women were also instructed in 'needle wisdom,' a skill Sally demonstrated with proficiency. "I have set a stocking on the needles, and intend to be mighty industrious." Though certainly a member of the privileged class, mundane household tasks did not escape her. "Rose at half-past four this morning. Iron'd industriously till one o'clock, din'd, went up stairs, threw myself on the bed, and fell asleep."

One of the more delightful and touching aspects of Sally's journal are her encounters with the young American military officer, William Stoddert (spelled "Stodard" in Sally's journal). The nineteen-year-old Stoddert served as Major of Brigade in the Maryland Battalion to his uncle, General Smallwood. Sally was clearly enamored from her first meeting with the dashing young Major. "Well, here comes the glory, the Major, so bashful, so famous, &c . . . he is large in his person, manly, and an engaging countenance and address." The relationship between the Major and the colonial Quaker girl, however, never developed. As fate would have it, Stoddert returned to Maryland after the war, married, and died at the age of 34 in 1793.

Throughout Sally's diary, we catch glimpses of major historical figures and events occurring at that time. During the nine months she wrote the journal, from September 25, 1777 to June 20, 1778, the British captured Philadelphia (". . . cousin Jesse heard that Gen. Howe's army had moved down towards Philadelphia"); the Colonial Army was defeated at Germantown ("The battle of Germantown, and the horrors of that day, are recent in my mind"); and Washington and his Army suffered through a horrendous winter at Valley Forge ("General Washington's army have gone into winter quarters at Valley Forge").

Sally Wister was born in Philadelphia on July 20, 1761 at the family residence on Market Street, home to the city's wealthy elite. Sally and her family returned to their home in Philadelphia in July 1778 after the British had evacuated the city. She never married and spent her life in solitude primarily occupied with religious matters. She died on April 25, 1804 at the age of 42.

For some inexplicable reason, Deborah Norris never saw the journal until 1830, twenty-six years after Sally's death. In returning the journal to Sally's brother Charles Wister, Deborah wrote that she "returns the manuscript which he kindly lent her some time ago, and which has, together with the memory of the beloved writer, brought vividly to her mind days long since past."

℘ *Journal of Sally Wister* ℘

To Deborah Norris:

Tho' I have not the least shadow of an opportunity to send a letter, if I do write, I will keep a sort of journal of the time that may expire before I see thee: the perusal of it may some time hence give pleasure in a solitary hour to thee and our Sally Jones.

Yesterday, which was the 24th of September, two Virginia officers call'd at our house, and inform'd us that the British Army had cross'd the Schuylkill. Presently after, another person stopp'd, and confirm'd what they had said, and that Gen'l Washington and Army were near Pottsgrove. Well, thee may be sure we were sufficiently scared; however, the road was very still till evening.

About seven o'clock we heard a great noise. To the door we all went. A large number of waggons, with about three hundred of the Philadelphia Militia. They begged for drink, and several push'd into the house. One of those that entered was a little tipsy, and had a mind to be saucy.

I then thought it time for me to retreat; so figure me (mightily scar'd, as not having presence of mind enough to face so many of the Military), running in at one door, and out another, all in a shake with fear; but after a while, seeing the officers appear gentlemanly; and the soldiers civil, I call'd reason to my aid. My fears were in some measure dispell'd, tho' my teeth rattled, and my hand shook like an aspen leaf. They did not offer to take their quarters with us; so, with many blessings, and as many adieus, they marched off.

I have given thee the most material occurrences of yesterday faithfully.

℘℘

Fourth Day, September 25th.

This day, till twelve o'clock, the road was mighty quiet, when Hobson Jones came riding along. About that time he made a stop at our door, and said that the British were at Skippack road; that we should soon see their light horse, and [that] a party of Hessians had actually turn'd into our lane. My Dadda and Mamma gave it the credit it deserv'd, for he does not keep strictly to the truth in all respects; but the delicate, chicken-hearted Liddy and I were wretchedly scar'd. We cou'd say nothing but "Oh! what shall we do? What will become of us?" These questions only augmented the terror we were in.

Well, the fright went off. We saw no light horse or Hessians. . . .

Wister, Sarah. (1902). *Sally Wister's journal, a true narrative; being a Quaker maiden's account of her experiences with officers of the Continental army, 1777–1778*, Philadelphia: Ferris & Leach.

ဆာ

Fifth Day, September 26th.

... About twelve o'clock, cousin Jesse heard that Gen. Howe's army had moved down towards Philadelphia. Then, my dear, our hopes & fears were engaged for you. However, my advice is, summon up all your resolution, call Fortitude to your aid, and don't suffer your spirits to sink, my dear; there's nothing like courage; 'tis what I stand in need of myself, but unfortunately have little of it in my composition.

I was standing in the kitchen about 12, when somebody came to me in a hurry, screaming, "Sally, Sally, here are the light horse!" This was by far the greatest fright I had endured; fear tack'd wings to my feet; I was at the house in a moment; at the porch I stopt, and it really was the light horse.

I ran immediately to the western door, where the family were assembled, anxiously waiting for the event. They rode up to the door and halted, and enquired if we had horses to sell; he was answer'd negatively.

"Have not you, sir," to my father, "two black horses?"

"Yes, but have no mind to dispose of them."

My terror had by this time nearly subsided. The officer and men behav'd perfectly civil; the first drank two glasses of wine, rode away, bidding his men follow, which, after adieus in number, they did. The officer was Lieutenant Lindsay, of Bland's regiment, Lee's troop. The men, to our great joy, were Americans, and but 4 in all. What made us imagine them British, they wore blue and red, which with us is not common.

It has rained all this afternoon, and to present appearances, will all night. In all probability the English will take possession of the city to-morrow or next day. What a change will it be! May the Almighty take you under His protection, for without His divine aid all human assistance is vain. ...

Nothing worth relating has occurred this afternoon. Now for trifles. I have set a stocking on the needles, and intend to be mighty industrious. This evening some of our folks heard a very heavy cannon. We supposed it to be fir'd by the English. The report seem'd to come from Philad[a]. We hear the American army will be within five miles of us tonight.

The uncertainty of our position engrosses me quite. Perhaps to be in the midst of war, and ruin, and the clang of arms. But we must hope the best.

Here, my dear, passes an interval of several weeks, in which nothing happen'd worth the time and paper it wou'd take to write it. The English, however, in the interim, had taken possession of the city.

ဆာ

Second Day, October the 19th, 1777.

Now for new and uncommon scenes. As I was lying in bed, and ruminating on past and present events, and thinking how happy I shou'd be if I cou'd see you, Liddy came running into the room, and said there was the greatest drumming, fifing, and rattling of waggons that ever she had heard. What to make of this we were at a loss. We dress'd and down stairs in a hurry. Our wonder ceas'd.

The British had left Germantown, and our army was marching to take possession. It was the general opinion that they wou'd evacuate the capital. Sister Betsy and myself, and G. E. went about half a mile from home, where we cou'd see the army pass. . . .

Several officers call'd to get some refreshment, but none of consequence till this afternoon. Cousin Prissa and myself were sitting at the door; I in a green skirt, dark short gown, &c. Two genteel men of the military order rode up to the door: "Your servants, ladies," &c; ask'd if they could have quarters for Genl. Smallwood. Aunt Foulke thought she cou'd accommodate them as well as most of her neighbours,—said they could. One of the officers dismounted, and wrote

SMALLWOOD'S QUARTERS

over the door, which secured us from straggling soldiers. After this he mounted his steed and rode away.

When we were alone our dress and lips were put in order for conquest, and the hopes of adventures gave brightness to each before passive countenance. . . .

In the evening his Generalship came with six attendants, which compos'd his family, a large guard of soldiers, a number of horses and baggage-waggons. The yard and house were in confusion, and glitter'd with military equipments.

Gould was intimate with Smallwood, and had gone into Jesse's to see him. While he was there, there was a great running up and down stairs, so I had an opportunity of seeing and being seen, the former most agreeable, to be sure. One person, in particular, attracted my notice. He appear'd cross and reserv'd; but thee shall see how agreeably disappointed I was. . . .

How new is our situation! I feel in good spirits, though surrounded by an Army, the house full of officers, the yard alive with soldiers,—very peaceable sort of men, tho'. They eat like other folks, talk like them, and behave themselves with elegance; so I will not be afraid of them, that I won't.

Adieu. I am going to my chamber to dream, I suppose, of bayonets and swords, sashes, guns, and epaulets.

ကာ

Third Day Morn., October 20th.

I dare say thee is impatient to know my sentiments of the officers; so, while Somnus embraces them, and the house is still, take their characters according to their rank.

The General is tall, portly, well made: a truly martial air, the behaviour and manner of a gentleman, a good understanding, & great humanity of disposition, constitute the character of Smallwood. . . .

Well, here comes the glory, the Major, so bashful, so famous, &c. He shou'd come before the Captain, but never mind. I at first thought the Major cross and proud, but I was mistaken. He is about nineteen, nephew to the Gen'l, and acts as Major of brigade to him; he cannot be extoll'd for the graces of person, but for those of the mind he may justly be celebrated; he is large in his person, manly, and an engaging countenance and address.

∞☯

Fourth-Day, Oct. 21st.

. . . I have heard strange things of the Major. Worth a fortune of thirty thousand pounds, independent of anybody; the Major, moreover, is vastly bashful; so much so he can hardly look at the ladies. (Excuse me., good sir; I really thought you were not clever; if 'tis bashfulness only, we will drive that away.)

Fifth-day, Sixth-day, and Seventh-day pass'd. The Gen'l still here; the Major still bashful.

∞☯

Third Day Eve., October 27th.

We had again the pleasure of the Gen'l and suite at afternoon tea. He (the Gen'l, I mean) is most agreeable; so lively, so free, and chats so gaily, that I have quite an esteem for him. I must steel my heart! Capt. Furnival is gone to Baltimore, the residence of his belov'd wife.

The Major and I had a little chat to ourselves this eve. No harm, I assure you thee: he and I are friends. . . .

∞☯

Second Day Morn, November 1st.

To-day the Militia marches, and the Gen'l and officers leave us. Heigh ho! I am very sorry; for when you have been with agreeable people, 'tis impossible not to feel regret when they bid you adieu, perhaps forever. When they leave us we shall be immur'd in solitude.

The Major looks dull.

About two o'clock the Gen. and Major came to bid us adieu. With daddy and mammy they shook hands very friendly; to us they bow'd politely.

Our hearts were full. I thought Major was affected.

"Good-bye, Miss Sally," spoken very low. He walk'd hastily and mounted his horse. They promised to visit us soon.

We stood at the door to take a last look, all of us very sober.

The Major turn'd his horse's head, and rode back, dismounted.

"I have forgot my pistols," pass'd us, and ran upstairs.

He came swiftly back to us, as if wishing, through inclination, to stay; by duty compell'd to go. He remounted his horse.

"Farewell, ladies, till I see you again," and canter'd away.

We look'd at him till the turn in the road hid him from our sight. "Amiable major," "Clever fellow," "Good young man," was echo'd from one to the other. I wonder whether we shall ever see him again. He has our wishes for his safety. . . .

℘Q

December 5th, Sixth Day.

Oh, gracious! Debbie, I am all alive with fear. The English have come out to attack (as we imagine) our army. They are on Chestnut Hill, our army three miles this side. What will become of us, only six miles distant?

We are in hourly expectation of an engagement. I fear we shall be in the midst of it. Heaven defend us from so dreadful a sight. The battle of Germantown, and the horrors of that day, are recent in my mind. It will be sufficiently dreadful if we are only in hearing of the firing, to think how many of our fellow-creatures are plung'd into the boundless ocean of eternity, few of them prepar'd to meet their fate. But they are summon'd before an all-merciful Judge, from whom they have a great deal to hope.

℘Q

Seventh Day, December 6th.

No firing this morn. I hope for one more quiet day.

℘Q

Seventh Day; 4 o'clock

I was much alarm'd just now, sitting in the parlour, indulging melancholy reflections, when somebody burst open the door, "Sally, here's Major Stodard!"

I jumped. Our conjectures were various concerning his coming. The poor fellow, from great fatigue and want of rest, together with being expos'd to the night air, had caught cold, which brought on a fever. He cou'd scarcely walk, and I went into aunt's to see him.

I was surpris'd. Instead of the lively, alert, blooming Stodard, who was on his feet the instant we enter'd, he look'd pale, thin, and dejected, too weak to rise. A bow, and "How are you, Miss Sally?"

"How does thee do, Major?"

I seated myself near him, inquir'd the cause of his indisposition, ask'd for the Gen'l, receiv'd his compliments. Not willing to fatigue him with too much chat, I bid him adieu.

To-night Aunt Hannah Foulke, Senr, administer'd something. Jesse assisted him to his chamber. He had not lain down five minutes before he was fast asleep. Adieu. I hope we shall enjoy a good night's rest.

℘)ᖇ

First Day Morn, December 7th.

I trip'd into aunt's. There sat the Major, rather more like himself. How natural it was to see him.

"Good morning, Miss Sally."

"Good morrow, Major, how does thee do to-day?"

Major: "I feel quite recover'd."

Sally: "Well, I fancy this indisposition has sav'd thy head this time."

Major: "No, ma'am; for if I hear a firing, I shall soon be with them." That was heroic.

About eleven, I dress'd myself, silk and cotton gown. It is made without an apron. I feel quite awkwardish, and prefer the girlish dress.

℘)ᖇ

Fifth Day, December 11th.

Our Army mov'd, as we thought, to go into winter quarters, but we hear there is a party of the enemy gone over Schuylkill; so our Army went to look at them.

I observ'd to Stodard, "So you are going to leave us to the English."

"Yes, ha! ha! ha! leave you for the English."

He has a certain indifference about him sometimes that to strangers is not very pleasing. He sometimes is silent for minutes. One of these silent fits was interrupted the other day by his clasping his hands and exclaiming aloud, "Oh, my God, I wish this war was at an end!"

℘)ᖇ

Seventh-day, December 20th.

General Washington's army have gone into winter quarters at Valley Forge.

We shall not see many of the military now. We shall be very intimate with solitude. I am afraid stupidity will be a frequent guest.

After so much company, I can't relish the idea of sequestration.

૪૭૦૨

First-day Night.

A dull round of the same thing over again. I shall hang up my pen till something offers worth relating.

૪૭૦૨

May 11th, 1778

The scarcity of paper, which is very great in this part of the country, and the three last months producing hardly anything material, has prevented me from keeping a regular account of things; but to-day the scene begins to brighten, and I will continue my nonsense.

૪૭૦૨

June 3, Six o'clock, Even^g.

. . . A horseman deliver'd this message: "Let the troop lie on their arms, and be ready to march at a moment's warning."

He immediately gave those orders to the sergeant. Every soldier was in motion. I was a good deal frighted'd, and ask'd Watts the reason. He fancy'd the British were in motion, tho' he had not receiv'd such intelligence.

"What will thee do if they come here?"

"Defend the house as long as I can, ma'am."

I was shock'd. "Bless my heart; what *will* become of us?"

"You may be very safe. The house is an excellent house to defend; only do you be still. If the British vanquish us, down on your knees, and cry, 'Bless the king.' If we conquer them, why, you know you are safe."

૪૭૦૨

Sixth Day, June 5th, Morn, 11 o'clock.

Last night we were a little alarm'd. I was awaken'd about 12 o'clock with somebody's opening the chamber door. I observ'd Cousin Prissa talking to Mamma. I asked what was the matter.

"Only a party of light horse."

"Are they Americans?" I quickly said.

She answer'd in the affirmative (which dispell'd my fears), and told me Major Jameson commanded, and that Capts. Call and Nixon were with him. With this intelligence she left us, and I revolved in my mind whether or not Jameson would renew his acquaintance; but Morpheus buried all my ideas, and this morn I rose by or near seven, dress'd in my light chintz, which is made gown-fashion, kenting handkerchief, and linen apron.

"Sufficiently smart for a country girl, Sally."

Don't call me a country girl, Debby Norris. Please to observe that I pride myself upon being a Philadelphian, and that a residence of 20 months has not at all diminished the love I have for that dear place; and as soon as one very capital altercation takes place (which is very much talk'd of at present), I expect to return to it with a double pleasure. . . .

℘)℃

First Day, Even'g

. . . The occurrences of the day come now. I left my chamber between eight and nine, breakfasted, went up to dress, put on a new purple and white striped Persian, white petticoat, muslin apron, gauze cap, and handkerchief. Thus array'd, Miss Norris, I ask your opinion. Thy partiality to thy friend will bid thee say I made a tolerable appearance. Not so, my dear. I was this identical Sally Wister, with all her whims and follies; and they have gain'd so great an ascendancy over my prudence, that I fear it will be a hard matter to divest myself of them. But I will hope for a reformation.

℘)℃

Fifth Day Night, June 18th.

Rose at half-past four this morning. Iron'd industriously till one o'clock, din'd, went up stairs, threw myself on the bed, and fell asleep. About four sister Hannah waked me, and said uncle and Foulks were down stairs; so I decorated myself, and went down. Felt quite lackadaisical. However, I jump'd about a little, and the stupid fit went off.

We have had strange reports about the British being about to leave Philad[a]. I can't believe it. Adieu.

℘)℃

Sixth Day Morn, June 19th.

We have heard an astonishing piece of news!—that the English have entirely left the city! It is almost impossible! Stay, I shall hear further.

ℬↃႦ

Sixth Day Eve.

A light horseman has just confirm'd the above intelligence! This is *charmante*! They decamp'd yesterday. He (the horseman) was in Philad^a. It is true. They have gone. Past a doubt. I can't help forbear exclaiming to the girls, -

"Now are you sure the news is true? Now are you sure they have gone?"

"Yes, yes, yes!" they all cry, "and may they never return."

Dr. Gould came here to-night. Our army are about six miles off, on their march to the Jerseys.

ℬↃႦ

Seventh Day Morn.

O.F. arrived just now, and relateth as *followeth:*—The Army began their march at six this morn by their house. Our worthy Gen'l Smallwood breakfasted at Uncle Caleb's. He ask'd how Mr. & Mrs. Wister and the young ladies were, and sent his respects to us.

Our brave, our heroic General Washington was escorted by fifty of the Life Guard, with drawn swords. Each day he acquires an addition to his goodness.

We have been very anxious to hear how the inhabitants have far'd. I understand that Gen'l Arnold, who bears a good character, has command of the city, and the soldiers conducted with great decorum. Smallwood says that they had the strictest orders to behave well; and I dare say they obey'd the order. I now think of nothing but returning to Philadelphia.

So shall now conclude this journal with humbly hoping that the Great Disposer of events, who has graciously vouchsaf'd to protect us to this day through many dangers, will still be pleas'd to continue his protection.

Sally Wister.

North Wales, June 20th, 1778.

In the Classroom

Chronological Thinking

- Create a time line of the major events in the Revolutionary War mentioned in Sally's journal.
- Trace and document Sally's opinion of Major Stodard through the course of her diary.

Historical Comprehension

- Uncover evidence in Sally's journal that reveals which side she and her family supported.
- Locate on a historical map the sites Sally mentions in her journal.

Historical Analysis and Interpretation

- Write a letter to Sally in which you describe the events depicted in her journal from the perspective of a British sympathizer.
- Develop a Venn diagram indicating the manners and etiquette expected of young women in Colonial America and today, noting behaviors common to both eras.

Historical Research Capabilities

- Potential Topics:

  Religious Society of Friends   British capture of Philadelphia
  Battle of Germantown   Valley Forge
  Colonial crafts   Hessian Troops

Historical Issues-Analysis and Decision-Making

- Locate evidence in Sally's journal of how she and her family supported the American cause, and describe the potential consequences of such action.
- Identify the causes of the American Revolution from the diary and secondary sources.

3

The American Revolution: The Diary of David How

"This Day I Listed With Serg.^t Barker for one year—" At seventeen years of age, David How was already an experienced veteran at the time of his enlistment in the Continental Army on December 27, 1775. He had answered when the Minutemen had called him earlier in April. At the Battle of Bunker Hill in June, young How took aim and fired his musket just as the soldier next to him was shot down. Within seconds, How took his comrade's gun and fired at the advancing enemy. He quickly became one of America's nameless soldiers in the Revolutionary War.

Fortunately, *The Diary of David How* presents a very different picture of the American Revolution than does Sally Wister's journal; the two voices could not have been more dissimilar. Sally was from the privileged elite, part of Philadelphia's wealthy upper class. David came from a simple, uneducated country background, the third child in a family of ten. The American Revolution in Sally's journal is one of generals and colonels, tea and socializing. In David's diary, the war is witnessed through the eyes of a common soldier: the routine of daily army life; the effort to instill order on an undisciplined army; and the fight to survive disease and enemy fire.

His entries describe the daily life of a Revolutionary War soldier revealing much time spent on very mundane tasks. "I Cooked This Day." "This Day we have ben washing Our things." David also spent considerable time and effort seeking means to supplant his meager army wages, possibly foretelling his future as a successful merchant. "I Sold Jacob Osgood Blanket For two Dollars." "I Bought 7 Bushels of Chesnuts & give 4 pisterens per bushel." "Colonel Bricket paid me Eight Dolars for my gun."

During the war, discipline and punishment were swift and painful for those who disobeyed regulations. "There was four of Capt. Willey men Whept the first fifteen Stripes for deniing his Deuty." Minor transgressions based on today's standards were dealt with quite differently in the Continental Army. "This morning one of Capt. Pharinton's men was Whept 30 Lashes for Stealing A cheese."

What David felt and thought about the dangers he faced is difficult to determine. Although events are reported and described with little apparent emotion or reflection, the fact that they appear in his diary implies they held some significance. The two greatest threats to those serving in the Continental Army were disease ("Leut. Chandler Died with the Small pox At the pest house About one a Clock in the Day") and enemy fire ("Issac Fowls had His head Shot off with a Cannon Ball this morning").

The British evacuation of Boston; the battles of Long Island, Harlem Heights, Trenton, and Saratoga; Washington's crossing of the Delaware; Burgoyne's surrender: David How witnessed them all. He does not discuss military strategy or comment on the historical significance of these events. His concise, simple entries mirror exactly who he was: an uneducated, ordinary soldier doing the work that must be done.

David How was born in Methuen, Massachusetts in 1758, the third in a family of ten children. After the war, How began and built a successful career as a currier in Haverhill, Massachusetts. He was the first to engage in the wholesale manufacture of shoes in Haverhill, and was the very first who manufactured them in large quantities. His fellow-townspeople thought so highly of him that he was elected to the Massachusetts State Legislature, where he served for twelve years. Mr. How died on February 9, 1842 at the age of 85.

๛ *Diary of David How* ๙

DIARY.

Dec^{mb} 27^d 1775   This Day I Listed With Serg.^t Barker for one year—

28^d   There went a bought 12 Hundred men Down to Cobble Hill In the Night In order To go over to Bunker Hill, but The Ice want Strong a nuf.

30   I Sold Jacob Osgood Blanket For two Dollars

How, David. (1865). *Diary of David How: A Private in Colonel Paul Dudley Sargent's Regiment of the Massachusetts Line, in the Army of the American Revolution.* Cambridge: H.O. Houghton and Company.

Jany th 8 1776   This Day I Began Work with Mr Watson. this Night our Soldiers wint over to Charles-town and Burnt up Eleven houses. took Six Prisoners. None killed

18^d   I went to Lexonton to Cutting Wood & Brought home a Load.

19^d   I went to Lexenton after a Load of wood and got home before Night

22 day   I Listed with Leut David Chandler in Coln. Sergant Regment

23d   I Cooked This Day

I Received one months pay of the Coln. and Twelve Shiling For a blanket

24 day   I Cook this Day & Bought 3 Barrels of Cyder for 9/ per Barrel

25 day   I Bought 7 Bushels of Chesnuts & give 4 pisterens per bushel

Jan 26   Colonel Bricket paid me Eight Dolars for my gun. I Sent home Sixteen Dollars by James Silver In a leter to methuen

27   We bought a wild Turcy that Weight 17 ¼ lb and had it for Supper.

30   I went to the Hospettal to See Stephen Barker, he is Sick of a feavour.— We have Sold Nuts and Cyder Every Day This weak.

31   I Bought 4 Bushels of Apels and gave 12s. pr Bushel for them.

[february] 8   I went to prospeck hill After I had done my Steant Running ball. In the Evening our men went Over to Charlestown & Burnt a mill there

13   I Bought a gun & Bayonet & Cateridge Box of Joseph Jackson and gave 42/6 Lawful Money for the Whole. I have ben Makeing Cateridges this Day.

14   This morning A Bout 4 Clock the Troops at Boston Landed At Docester hill and Burnt 4 or 5 Houses & Took one old man that Be long in them. Our people ware Soon A Larm^d & went Down And Drove them Back As fast a gin as they come.

21   Leu^t. Chandler Died with the Small pox At the pest house About one a Clock in the Day

28   I went to prospeck hill And cap^t Farnum Paid Eight pound Seventeen Shiling & Seven Pence Lawfull money that was due to me for My Service Last year   James How come here And Staid this Night.

March 3   Last Night there was Firiing Almost all Night on both Sides Two of our morters Splet in pices at Litchmors point; there Was a Shell Sent from Boston to prospeck hill This morning and fell on a platform in the Fort. I went to Litchmors point and Prospeck hill & winters hill To see Jonathan How. Our people are carrying Cannon to Roxbury & to Litchmors point

FIGURE 3.1   Colonial soldiers engaged in battle. Photograph of a diorama in the Milwaukee Public Museum. (Library of Congress, Prints & Photographs Division, Detroit Publishing Company Collection, LC-D413-1).

4   Last Night there was Afireing all Night with Cannan and morters on both Sides; our people Splet The Congress the Third Time that they fireed it. Three Regments went From Cambridge to Roxbury & carried Some Field Pieces with them. The milisher from Several towns are Called In to Stay 3 Days.

17. B 1776   This morning about Nine a clock there was A Larem and our people Hear went into the boats For to go to Boston & gnrael Sulliven With a party of men Went to Bunker hill & Took posesien of it.

This afternoon I went Down to charlestown neck In order to go over to Bunker hill But the Sentinals Stopt me

27   There was four of Capt. Willey men Whept the first fifteen Stripes for den;ing his Deuty the 2^d 39 Stripes For Stealing & Deserting 3^d 10 Lashes for get;ing Drunk & Dening Duty 4^d 20 Lashes Deniing his Duty & geting Drunk.

A most all the kings Ships Saild off this After noon.

April 2   This morning one of Capt. Pharinton's men was Whept 30 Lashes for Stealing A cheese.

Our Regment all marched over to Bunker Hill and Staid there this Night In the Fort.

May 12   There was one two of The Kings Ships come in Sight & was 24 guns fired from the Ships

May 13   This after Noon went Down to Long Island with Two boats and the kings Ships fireed three guns at Us as we come a crost From Long Island to Pudden point from pudden point we come to the Castle.

August 19   This day at 12 a Clock we went on board a Sloop and set Sail for Newlondon and got Half Down there and Ran a ground and staid all Night

20   This morning we set Sail And got to New London at Noon—and Staid ther at night

21   This morning we set sail for Newyor but the wind being Contrary we were obliged to come To anchor at night.

27   This morning we got to Horns Hook whare we found The rest of our Regement Stationed.—About 6 Miles from the City of N.york.
Our Army on long Island Have ben Engaged in battle With the Enimy and Kill^d And taken a good many on Both sides.

29   This night our army on long Island All left it & Brought all there Bagage to N. York.

Septem 2   We be gun a fort hear Gnral Washington has Ben here at the fort This Day.

8   This morning there be gan A very hot fire from a Battery Erected Right Oppiset To our fort—and they Killed Corp Hadua of Capt Perry's Comp^a The fire Was kept up on both Sides very Brisk all Day

9   There has ben a very heavy Fire on Both Sides with Cannon and Morters all day.

10   The fire has ben kept Up on both Sides with Shells And Cannon

11   We all have been on for teag this day. The fireing has ben kept up All Day with Bums & Balls.

12   Issac Fowls had His head Shot off with a Cannon Ball this morning.

15   This morning the Enimy on Long Island—Crossed to Turcle Bay and Landed on York Island Our people thought best to Leave the lower part of the Town so that the Shipping Might not play on us. Our army all marchd to the upper part of the Town this after Noon.

16   Some part of our Army Had a Smart fight with The Enimy in Harlem Woods—Our Army Drove them And Killed a Grate many On Both Sides—Bennoni Was Killed in the Aaction

27   This Day Robbard Higings was Whipt 20 Lashes For geting Drunk and Dening Duty Thomas Brimblecom was whipt 10 Lashes For geting Drunk The Drummayjor was whipt 15 lashes for Theft.

28   I have ben to Kings Bridge

29   Serj^t Duley Noyce Went With a party of Men to the Orderly Store to Running of Balls
    Mr. John Adams has ben hear this Day.

December 24   We have ben Drawing Cateridges And provisions in order for a Scout.

25   This Day at 12 aClock we March^d Down the River about 12 miles. in the Night we Crossed the River Dullerway With a large Body of men And Field Pieces.

26   This morning at 4 aClock We set off with our Field pieces Marchd 8 miles to Trenton Whare we ware Atacked by a Number of Hushing & we Toock 1000 of them besides killed Some Then we march^d back And got to the River at Night And got over all the Hushing

27   This morning we Crossed the River and Come to our Camp At Noon

28   This Day we have ben washing Our things.

29   This Day we Draw^d Provision And Coock it in order for a March and at Night we all March^d to Howles Ferry And Crossed it and Staid there Till morning

30   This morning we march^d to Trenton with all our Baggage

31   The Gnrl ordered all to parade And see How many wood Stay 6 Weaks Longer and a Grate Part of the Army Stays for that time

January 1   This fore noon we have been Drawing our wages & Sase money. This after Noon we set out For New England march^d 4 miles Staid at Night there

[January] 15   This day I march^d to Methuen and Got to Fathers at Night

๛ *David How's Second Diary* ๛

Sept 29 1777   This Day Between 40 & 50 men ware Called for to march to Genl Gates is assistance From Methuen And I Turned out as one of the Number.

30   I went to Andover to Mr. Johnson's after A Pair of Shoes for the march.

October 1   I have ben makeing Cateridge in order for The march

2   This morning we all Set out for the march

11.   This morning we march To Salletogo where we Stopt and Draw^d provisions

12.   This morning we had Orders to Send our horses Back and March to Fort Edward and at Noon we Crossed Burtin Kill River and got to Fort Edward at Night And camped in the woods. I went on gard this Night

13   This Day we have ben Building us Camps And Drawing provisions

14   This Day our Scouts Took And brought in a Number of Regulars and Tores

15   This morning our Scouts Brought in upwards of 50 Indians that ware made prisoners Yestoday Near Fort George. They had With them Silver & Gold And a Number of Blankets And other Valuable Bagege.

16   This morning we had orders To march from Fort Edward to Burting Kill And got ther at Night

17   This morning we march^d To Salletoga with all the Reg^t And at 10 oClock the British Troops under the Command of Gnrl Burgoin All Lay Down there Arams And march^d to our lines As prisoners of war. This after noon we Draw^d 4 Days provisions In Order for a march

18   This morning we all March^d to Stillwater got There in the afternoon And In Camped there The Enimy have ben Crossing the river this Day

19   This Day we have ben fixing For a march and at noon we Set out with the prisoners for to Guard them to Boston and at Night we all Stopt And Encamped Tulls Mills

Nove^{br} 1   This Day we have Ben waiting for the Prisoner all to Get together & Draw provisions

2   This morning we Set off. march^d through Spenser & Lester and at Night we Satid at Worster.

6   Day we march^d through Watertown and Cambridge And march^d To Prospeck Hill and Left all the prisoners And ware all Dismissed And we march^d to Menotomy, Staid at Night
    Its ben Very Rainney all Day.

7   This morning we Set out For Home march^d through Whoburn & Wilmenton And Andover & Got to Methuen at Night—

*In the Classroom*_____

Chronological Thinking

- Identify the technology and tools that exist today that would have made David's life easier.
- Match the dates in David's diary with events on a time line of the Revolutionary War.

Historical Comprehension

- Write a letter from David's perspective home to his mother that describes life in the Continental Army.
- Write a narrative in which you hypothesize as to why David joined the Continental Army.

Historical Analysis and Interpretation

- Compare life in the Continental Army with that of life in the armed forces today. For information on the latter, use sources such as newspapers, the Internet, interviews with family members, and so on.
- Construct a poster enticing new recruits to join the Continental Army.

Historical Research Capabilities

- Potential Topics:

Lexington and Concord	Battle of Bunker Hill
Minute Men	Battle of Trenton
Battle of Saratoga	Continental Army

Historical Issues-Analysis and Decision-Making

- Analyze the difficulties faced by colonists living under British rule.
- Assess alternatives the colonists possessed, short of war, to solve their problems.

4

The Industrial Revolution: The Letters of Mary Paul

It began with an act of espionage. Britain's industrial revolution had been underway for some time when prominent Boston merchant Francis Cabot Lowell visited Manchester, England in 1811 to study the manufacturing of textiles. Fear of competition had led Britain to enact strict laws forbidding the export of machinery and technical drawings. Lowell, however, was able to commit details of Britain's textile machinery to memory. The power looms he constructed on his return home were superior to even those of the British. For the first time, the process of making cloth could be completed entirely under one roof, from the cleaning of the cotton to the printing of the cloth in the textile factory Lowell's Boston Manufacturing Company built on the banks of the Charles River in Waltham, Massachusetts in 1814. America's Industrial Revolution had begun.

Lowell's venture was so successful that he and his partners sought a location to expand operations. A site was selected on the Merrimack River in what was then Chelmsford, Massachusetts because it possessed the necessary waterpower to operate the looms and other machinery. The town that now bears his name was incorporated in 1826 with a population of 2,500. By the time the author of the letters contained in this chapter, Mary Paul, arrived in 1845 to work in the mills, Lowell's population had increased to almost 30,000.

Mary Paul, the only daughter of Bela Paul, was a young woman of fifteen from northern Vermont. While mill wages were not sufficient to lure men off their New England farms, young women were attracted by a decent income ("I could earn much more to begin with than I can anywhere about here"), independent living, and the cultural opportunities not available in rural settings.

A system of company-owned boardinghouses was established to ease the fears of reluctant parents and maintain the necessary flow of workers. "I have a very good boarding place, have enough to eat and that which is good enough. the girls are all kind and obliging." The boardinghouse keeper was a corporation employee and was responsible for the physical, moral, and spiritual health of the 30–40 young women under her supervision. All meals were taken at the boardinghouse, doors were locked and visitors prohibited after 10:00 pm, and church attendance was mandatory.

Mary's work day was thirteen hours long. "At 5 o'clock in the morning the bell rings for the folks to get up and get breakfast at half past six it rings for the girls to get up and at seven they are called into the mill, at half past 12 we have dinner, are called back again at one and stay till half past seven." On Saturdays she worked eight hours. Mary earned a total of $1.65 for the 73 hours she worked each week and $1.17 went for board. Work in the mills was dangerous and accidents frequently occurred. "Last Thursday one girl fell down and broke her neck which caused instant death."

Mary's transformation from satisfied mill worker to disgruntled employee took slightly less than three years. In the same letter in which she writes of her schedule, income, and working conditions, Mary expresses satisfaction with her life in the mills. "I think that the factory is the best place for me and if any girl wants employment I advise them to come to Lowell." In a letter dated November 5, 1848, however, Mary conveys very different feelings to her father about work in the mills. "It is very hard indeed and sometimes I think I shall not be able to endure it—I have never worked so hard in my life." Many mill workers went through similar changes in attitude.

Family was obviously important to Mary Paul. In the numerous letters she wrote her father, Mary frequently expressed concern about his health ("It troubles me very much, the thought of your being lame so much and alone too. If there were any way that I could make it expedient, I would go back to Claremont myself") and shared news about her three brothers: Henry, Julius, and William ("He is still in the Prison and will probably remain there until a better situation offers").

Mary worked briefly as a seamstress after leaving Lowell. In the final letter published here, like in the first, Mary writes her father seeking permission to move, this time to a utopian community called the North American Phalanx. Not long after that experiment failed, Mary wed Isaac Guild, the son of her former Lowell boardinghouse keeper, in 1857. The couple moved to Lynn, Massachusetts where Mary's two children were born. Mary Paul's correspondence with her father ended with his death in 1863 and with it, our source of information about the rest of her life.

ℬ *Mary S. Paul Letters* ℛ

Saturday, September 13th, 1845

Dear Father

I received your letter this afternoon by Wm. Griffith. You wished me to write if I had seen Mr Angell. I have neither written to him nor seen him nor has he written to me. I began to write but could not write what I wanted to. I think if I could see him I could convince him of his error if he would let me talk. I am very glad you sent my shoes they fit very well indeed, they large enough every

    I want you to consent to me go to Lowell if you can. I think it would be much better for me than to stay about here. I could earn much more to begin with than I can anywhere about here. I am in need of clothes which I cannot get if I stay about here and for that reason I want to go to Lowell or some other place. We all think that if I could go with some steady girl that I might do well. I want you to think of it and make up your mind. Mercy Jane Griffith is going to start in four or five weeks. Aunt Miller and Aunt Sarah think it would be a good chance for me to go if you would consent which I want you to do if possible

    I want to see you and talk with you about it.

    Aunt Sarah gains slowly

Mary

Bela Paul

ℬℛ

Woodstock
November 8, 1845

Dear Father

As you wanted me to let you know when I am going to start for Lowell I improve this opportunity to write you   next Thursday, the 13th of this month is the day set on the Thursday afternoon   I should like to have you come

---

Mary Paul Letters, MSC-12, Vermont Historical Society

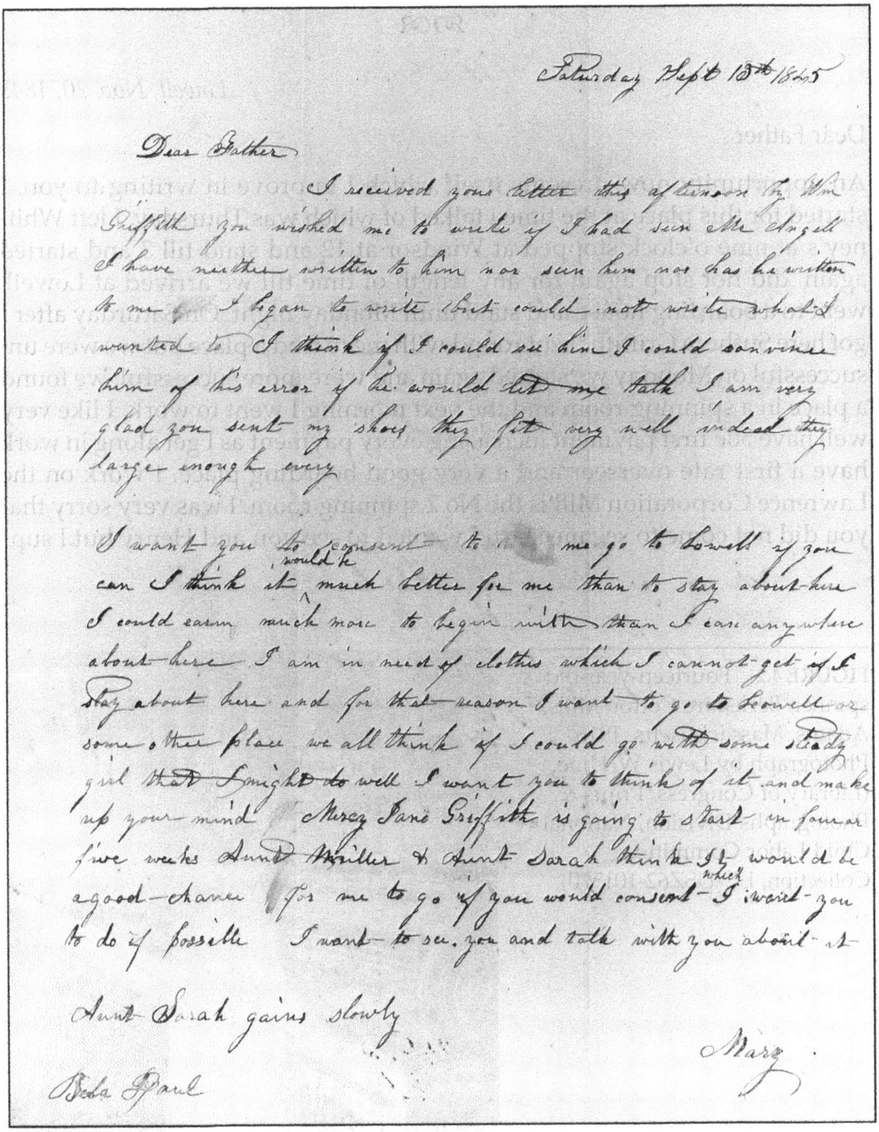

FIGURE 4.1 Letter from Mary Paul to her father, Bela, Saturday, September 13th, 1845. (Vermont Historical Society, MSC-12)

down if you come bring Henry if you can for I should like to see him before I go   Julius has got the money for me.

Yours Mary

℘)℘

Lowell, Nov. 20, 1845

Dear Father

An opportunity now presents itself which I improve in writing to you. I started for this place at the time I talked of which was Thursday. I left Whitney's at nine o'clock stopped at Windsor at 12 and staid till 3 and started again. did not stop again for any length of time till we arrived at Lowell. went to a boarding house and staid until Monday night. On Saturday after I got here Suthera Griffith went round with me to find a place but we were unsuccessful on Monday we started again and were more successful. we found a place in a spinning room and the next morning I went to work. I like very well have 50¢ first payment increasing every payment as I get along in work have a first rate overseer and a very good boarding place. I work on the Lawrence Corporation Mill is the No 2 spinning room. I was very sorry that you did not come to see me start. I wanted to see you and Henry but I sup-

FIGURE 4.2   Fourteen-year-old spinner, Berkshire Cotton Mills, Adams, Massachusetts, 1916. Photograph by Lewis W. Hine. (Library of Congress, Prints & Photographs Division, National Child Labor Committee Collection, LC-USZ62-101570).

pose that you were otherwise engaged. I hoped to see Julius but did not much expect to for I supposed he was engaged in other matters. He got six dollars for me which I was very glad of. It cost me $3.25 to come. stage fare was $3.00 and lodging at Windsor, 25 cts. had to pay only 25 cts for board for 2 days after I got here before I went into the mill. had 2.50 left with which I got a bonnet and some other small articles. Tell Harriet Burbank to send me paper. tell her I shall send her one as soon as possible. You must write as soon as you receive this. tell Henry I should like to hear from him. if you hear anything from William write for I want to know what he is doing. I shall write to uncle miller's folks the first opportunity. Aunt Nancy presented me with a new alpaca dress before I came away from there which I was very glad of. If think of staying here a year certain if not more I wish that you and Henry would come down here. I think that you might do well. I guess that Henry could get into the mill and I think that Julius might get in too. tell all friends that I should like to hear from them.

Excuse bad writing and mistakes
This from your loving daughter
Mary

PS be sure and direct to No 15 Lawrence Corporation
Bela Paul

Mary S Paul

℘)෬

Letter to Mr. Bela Paul

Lowell, Dec. 21st, 1845

Dear Father:

I received your letter on Thursday, the 14th with much pleasure. I am well which is one comfort. my life and health are spared while others are cut off. Last Thursday one girl fell down and broke her neck which caused instant death. she was going in or coming out of the mill and slipped down it being very icy the same day a man was killed by the cars, another had nearly all of his ribs broken, another was nearly killed by falling down and having a bale of cotton fall on him. last Tuesday we were paid in all I had six dollars and sixty cents paid $4.68 for board with the rest I got me a pair of rubbers and pair of 50 cts shoes, next payment I am to have a dollar week beside by board. we have not had much snow the deepest being not more than 4 inches. It has been very warm for winter perhaps you would like something about our regulations about going in and coming out of the mill. At 5 o'clock in the morning the bell rings for the folks to get up and get breakfast at half past six it rings for the girls to get up and at seven they are called into the mill, at half past 12 we have dinner, are called back again at one and stay till half past seven. I get along very well with my work. I can doff as fast as any girl in our room. I think I shall have frames before long. the usual time allowed for learning is six months but I think I shall have frames before I have been in three as I get along so fast. I think that the factory is the best place for me and if any girl wants employment I advise them to come to Lowell. Tell Harriet that although she does not hear from me she is not forgotten. I have so little time to devote to writing that I cannot write all I want to. there are half a dozen letters which I ought to write today but I have not time. tell Harriet I send my love to her and all of the girls. give my love to Mrs. Clement. tell Henry this will answer for him and you too for this time.

This from
Mary S Paul

Bela Paul
Henry S Paul

ဆၥလ

Letter from Mary Paul to her father Bela Paul

Lowell, April 12, 1846

Dear Father

I received your letter with much pleasure but was sorry to hear that you had been lame   I had waited a long time to hear from you but no letter came so last Sunday I thought I would write again which I did and was going to send it to the office Monday but at noon I received a letter from William so I did not send it at all. Last Friday I received a letter from you, you wanted to know what I am doing. I am at work in a Spinning room and tending four sides of warp which is one girl's work. The overseer tells me that he never had a girl get along better than I do and that he will do the best he can by me. I stand it well through though they tell me that I am growing very poor. I was paid nine shillings a week last payment and am to have more this one though we have been out considerable for back water which will take off a good deal. the agent promises to pay us nearly as much as we should have made but I do not think that he will. the payment was up last night and we are to be paid this week. I have a very good boarding place, have enough to eat and that which is good enough. the girls are all kind and obliging, the girls that I room with are all from Vermont and good girls, too. Now I will tell you about our rules at the boarding house. We have none in particular except that we have to go to bed about 10 o'clock. at half past four in the morning the bell rings for us to get up and at 5 for us to go into the mill. At seven we are called out to breakfast, are allowed half an hour between bells and the same at noon till the first of May when we have three-quarters till the first of September. we have dinner at half past 12 and supper at seven. if Julius should go to Boston tell him to come this way and see me. he must come to the Lawrence Counting room and call for me. he can ask some one to show him where the Lawrence is. I hope he will not fail to go. I forgot to tell you that I have not seen a particle of snow for six weeks and it is settled going. we have had a very mild winter but little snow. I saw Ann Hersey last Sunday. I did not know her until she told me who she was. I see the Griffith girls often. I received a letter from a girl in Bridgwater in which she told me that Mrs. Angell had heard some way that I could not get work and that she was much pleased and said that I was so bad that no one would have me. I believe I have written all so I will close for I have a letter to write to William this afternoon.

Yours affectionately
Mary S. Paul

Mr. Bela Paul

P.S. I give my love to all that inquire for me and tell them to write me a long letter. Tell Harriet I shall send her a paper

ᏕᎧᏇ

Letter from Mary Paul to her father, Bela Paul

Lowell, Nov 5th, 1848

Dear Father

Doubtless you have been looking for a letter from me all the weeks past—I would have written but wished to find whether I should be able to stand it to do the work that I am now doing. I was unable to get my old place in the cloth room on the Suffolk or any other corporation, next tried the dress rooms on the Lawrence Corner but did not succeed in getting a place. I almost concluded to give up and go back to Claremont but thought I would try once more so I went to my old overseer on the Tremont Corner. I had no idea that he would want me, but he did and I went to work last Tuesday—warping the same work I used to do.

It is very hard indeed and sometimes I think I shall not be able to endure it—I have never worked so hard in my life—but perhaps I shall get used to it—I shall try hard to do so—for there is no other work that I can do unless I spin and that I shall not undertake on any account—I presume you have heard before this that the wages are to be reduced on the 20th of this month—it is true and there seems to be a good deal of excitement on the subject but I cannot tell what will be the consequence. The companies pretend that they are losing

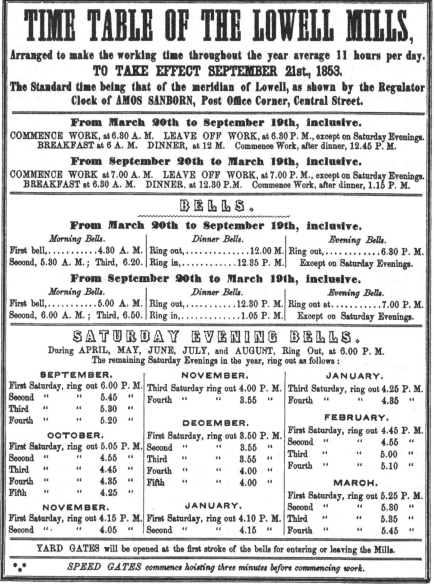

FIGURE 4.3   Time Table of the Lowell Mills, 1853. (American Textile History Museum, Lowell, Massachusetts, HD5107.L93 1853)

immense sums every day and therefore they are obliged to lessen the wages, but this seems perfectly absurd to me for they are constantly making <u>repairs</u> and it seems to me that this would not be if there were really any danger of their being obliged to <u>stop</u> the mills.

It is very difficult for any one to get into the mill on any corporation, all seem to be very full of help. I expect to be paid about two dollars a week but it will be dearly earned—I cannot tell how it is but never since I have worked in the mill have I been so very tired as I have for the last weeks but it may be owing to the long rest I have had for the last six months. I have not told you that I do not board on the Lawrence. The reason of this is because I wish to be nearer the mill, and I do not wish to pay the extra $12^{1/2}$ per week (I should not be obliged to do it if I boarded at 15) and I know that they are not able to give it to me, beside this I am so near I can go and see them as often as I wish, So considering all things I think I have done the best I could. I do not like her very well and am very sure I never shall as well as at Mother Guilds. I can now realise how very kind the whole family have ever been to me. It seems like going <u>home</u> when I go there which is every day. but now I see I have not yet told you where I do board. It is at No. 5 Tremont Corporation, please enlighten all who wish for information—There is one thing which I forgot to bring with me and which I want very much, that is my <u>rubbers</u>—they hand in the back room at uncle Jerrys—If Olive comes down here I presume you can send them by her— but if you should not have an opportunity to send them do not trouble yourself about them—There is another thing I wish to mention—about my fare down here—If you paid it all the way as I understood you did, there is something wrong about it—when we stopped at Concord to take the cars, I went to the ticket office to get a ticket which I knew I should be obliged to have—When I called for it I told the man that my fare was paid all the way and I wanted a ticket to Lowell, he told me if this was the case the Stage driver would get the ticket for me and I supposed of course he would,—but he <u>did not,</u> and when the ticket master called for my ticket in the <u>cars,</u> I was obliged to give him a dollar. Sometimes I have thought that the fare might <u>not</u> have been paid farther than Concord, if this is the case all is right but if it is not, then I have paid a dollar too much and gained the character of trying to cheat the company out of my fare, for the man thought I was lying to him I suppose. I want to know how it is and wish it could be settled for I do not like that <u>any</u> one should think <u>me</u> capable of such a thing even though that person be an utter stranger—but enough of this—

The Whigs of Lowell had a great time on the night of the 3rd. They had an immense procession of men on foot bearing <u>torches</u> and <u>banners</u> got up for the occasion—the houses were illuminated (Whig's houses) and by the way I should think the whole of <u>Lowell</u> were Whigs—I went out to see the illuminations and they did truly look splendid—The Merrimack house was illuminated from attic to cellar, every pane of glass in the house had a half candle to it and there were many others lighted in the same way—One entire block on the Minimus corner, with the exception of one tenement which doubtless was occupied by a Free Soiler who would not illuminate on any account whatever.

(Monday Eve) I have been to work today and think I shall manage to get along with the work. I am not so tired as I was last week—I have not yet found out what wages I shall get but presume that they shall be about $2.00 per week exclusive of board—I think of nothing further to write except I wish to prevail on Henry to write to me, also tell Olive to write and Evalina when she comes.

Give my love to uncle Jerry and aunt Betsey and tell little Lois that "Cousin Carra" thanks her very much for the apple she sent her—Her health is about the same that it was when she was at Claremont—No one has much hope of her ever being better.

> Write soon
> Yours Affectionately
> Mary L. Paul

Mr. Bela Paul

P.O. Do not forget to direct to No. 5 Tremont Cor. and tell all others to do the same.

ఎోఇఇ

Letter from Mary Paul to her father Bela Paul

Lowell, July 1st, 1849

Dear Father

I received your letter dated the 25th of June—on Wednesday—the 27th—and would have answered immediately but—I had not had time. I was very glad to get the letter from William—I had almost given up the hope of hearing from him and commenced a letter to him when yours came in which was his enclosed—I will give you his own words in regard to his health, etc.

"As for my own health, it has been generally very good, though for these last few days I have been quite unwell and was confined to my bed for a day or two. I feel quite unwell at this time." and of the Cholera he says, "It has broken out fearfully within a few days—on the 105h inst (June) there were 10 deaths from it, on the 11th—25, and I have not heard the report for yesterday (the 12th).

He is still in the Prison and will probably remain there until a better situation offers.

He says—"tell Henry I will write to him without fail before long."

My health has been pretty good though I have been obliged to be out of the mill four days—I thought <u>then</u> that it would be impossible for me to work through the hot weather but—<u>since,</u>—I think I shall manage to get through after a fashion. I do not know what wages I am to have as I have not yet been paid but shall not expect <u>much,</u> as I have not been able to do much although I have worked very hard—I shall send a letter with this to Evelina so that you can give it to her when you see her—Give my love to her when you see her—give my love to Henry and tell him I will write him as soon as I can and tell him to write me and not <u>wait</u> for <u>me.</u>

Yours affectionately
Mary S Paul

ഇ)രു

Letter from Mary Paul to her father, Bela Paul

Brattleboro, Nov. 27th, 1853

Dear Father

I think I will write you a few words tonight as you may be wishing to hear from me. Your letter of Nov. 13th tells me that you have been lame. I was sorry to hear it though I expected as much from your not writing before. It troubles me very much, the thought of your being lame so much and alone too. If there were any way that I could make it expedient, I would go back to Claremont myself and I sometimes I think I ought to do so—but the chance for me there is so <u>small,</u> and I can do so much better elsewhere that I have thought it was really better for me to be somewhere else but the thought of you always makes me wish to be where I can see you often—I feel anxious about Julius—I really wish that he might find steady employment at some good business—I am so sorry that he and Uncle Seth could not manage to agree—I wonder if he ever got the papers I sent him several weeks ago?

I have a plan for myself which I am going to lay before you and see what you think of it—When I was at Manchester last spring, my friend, Carrie and her husband were talking of going to New Jersey to live—and proposed that I should go with them. They have decided to go—and am thinking of going in a few weeks, maybe as soon as Jan. though they may not go until April or May—I have been thinking of it all summer, and have told them that I will go if you do not object—I can hardly get my own consent to go any farther away from you, though I know that in reality a few miles cannot make much difference—the name of the <u>town</u> is Atlantic, is about 40 miles from New York City. The people among whom they are going are

Associationists—the name will give you something of an idea of their principles. There about 125 persons in all that live there, and the Association is called the "North American Phalanx"—I presume that you may have heard of it. You have if you read the "Tribune". The editor "Mr. Greeley" is an associationist and a shareholder in the "Phalanx" but he does not live there — The advantage that will arise from my going there will be that I can get better pay without working so hard as at any other place. The price for work there being 9¢ an hour, and the number of hours for a day's work, <u>ten,</u> besides I should not be confined to one kind of work but could do almost anything, could have the privilege of doing anything that is done there, <u>Housework</u> if I chose and that without degrading myself, which is more than I could do anywhere else, that is, in the opinion of most people. A very foolish and <u>wrong</u> idea by the way—but one that has so much weight with girls, that they would live on 25 cts per week, at sewing, or school teaching, rather than work at housework. I would do it myself although I think it foolish.

This all comes from the way servants are <u>treated,</u> and I cannot see why girls can be blamed after all, for not wishing to "work out" as it is called. At the "Phalanx" it is different, <u>all</u> work there, and all are paid alike both men and women and have the <u>same pay</u> for the <u>same</u> work—There is no such word as <u>aristocracy</u> there unless there is real (not pretended) superiority, <u>that</u> will make itself <u>felt,</u> if not <u>acknowledged, everywhere.</u>

The <u>members</u> can live as <u>cheaply</u> as they choose as they pay only for what they <u>eat,</u> and no <u>profit</u> on that, most of the provisions being raised on the grounds—One can join them with or without funds, and can leave at any time they choose.

Frank has been there this Fall and was very much pleased with what he saw there and thought that it would be the best thing for Carrie and me to do with ourselves—A woman gets much better pay there than elsewhere, but it is not so with a man though he is not <u>meanly</u> paid by any means. There is more equality in such things according to the <u>work</u> not the sex, you know that men often get more than double the pay for doing the same work that women do—Carrie and Frank are both associationists and have been almost ever since I knew them, and I am acquainted with many others who are, and their principles are just what I would like to see carried into practice and they <u>are</u> as far as means will allow, at the Phalanx.

Another advantage from living there is this, the members can have privilege of <u>education</u> free of expense to themselves alone, the extent of this education must of course depend on the <u>means</u> of the society—If i could see you I could give you a better idea that I can possibly do by writing—but you will know something by this, enough to form an opinion perhaps and I wish you to let me know what you think of my plans—If you have any real objection as if you would rather I would not go so far away—let me know and I will cheerfully give up this idea of going—I hope sometime to be able to do something for you sometime. and sometimes I feel ashamed that I have not before this. I am not one of the <u>smart</u> kind, and never had a passion for laying up money, probably never shall have, can find ways enough to spend it though, (but I do not wish to be extravagant) Putting all these things together—I think explains the reason that I do not "lay up" anything, nothing more. I have never had very good pay—I am getting along slowly on coats and shall do better as I get more used to the business. I can work at my trade if I wish at the Phalanx—How are Uncle Jerry's family, give my love to them and Julius when you see him—I hope you will write me very soon as I shall be very anxious to know your mind and I wish to let Carrie know. If you should think it not for me to go I shall visit C—in the course of a few weeks. that is if we go in Jan. if not till April, I shall not probably come to C— until about that time. I have written you quite a long letter and it is not very plain—I am afraid you will never be able to read it—I ought to have written more plainly, but I am in something of a hurry and most offer that as my excuse. Write immediately please.

> *Affectionately yours*
> *Mary S Paul*

In the Classroom

Chronological Thinking

- Create a time line of significant events in America's Industrial Revolution from the letters and secondary sources.
- Provide specific evidence to show how Mary's attitude toward working in the mills changed during the course of her employment.

Historical Comprehension

- Write an imaginary newspaper account describing working conditions in the mills.
- Locate the major industrial centers during the period of Mary's letters on an historical map. Hypothesize the reasons for the selection of these sites.

Historical Analysis and Interpretation

- Write a letter to a mill owner from Mary's perspective in which you suggest ways to improve working conditions.
- Write a narrative describing what Mary's life would have been like had she chosen not to work in the mills.

Historical Research Capabilities

- Potential Topics:

Industrial Revolution	Francis Cabot Lowell
mill girls	child labor laws
utopian communities	textile industry

Historical Issues-Analysis and Decision-Making

- Analyze a young woman's options for education and employment in the early part of the nineteenth century.
- Identify and describe the historical events resulting in the increased employment options for women today.

5

The Overland Trail:
The Diary of
Sallie Hester

"The last hours were spent in bidding good bye to old friends. My mother is heartbroken over the separation of relatives and friends. . . . The last goodbye has been said—the last glimpse of our old home on the hill . . . and we are off." On March 20, 1849, fourteen-year-old Sallie Hester left her home in Indiana and became a participant in America's great migration west. The diary she left behind provides a detailed and descriptive account of her six-month journey.

Most emigrants were drawn west by newspaper accounts of fertile land and healthy climates, and slightly more than 18,000 emigrants traveled the Overland Trail to Oregon and California during the years 1840–1848. "My father is going in search of health," writes Sallie at the beginning of her diary. James Marshall's discovery of a pea-sized nugget of gold, however, just east of what is now Sacramento, California in 1848 permanently altered the landscape of the American west. When Sallie and her family made the overland trek the following year, so great were the numbers of emigrants on the trail that travel actually became congested. "As far as the eye can reach, so great is the emigration, you see nothing but wagons . . . a vast army on wheels."

Accidents, death, the availability of grass and water, and the condition of the trail are subjects Sallie returns to frequently throughout her diary; historians pay particular attention to the topics and events that appear on a recurring basis in a diary. These point out what was important both to the diarist and to the success of the endeavor being described.

"Our carriage upset at one place. All were thrown out, but no one was hurt." Accidents that befell the unlucky traveler meant a potentially disastrous delay or forced the emigrants to reverse course and head home. Death was a constant reminder of the perilous nature of the overland trip and is a recurring topic in many diary entries. "We had two deaths in our train within the past week of cholera—young men going West to seek their fortunes. We buried them on the banks of the Blue River, far from home and friends."

Steady progress and ultimately the success of the journey were dependent on the health and well-being of the animals pulling the wagon. Thus, access to grass and water and the shape of the trail occupied the minds of many traveling the Overland Trail. "Water and grass scarce. . . . Roads are rocky and trying to our wagons, and the dust is horrible."

Traveling with her family, Sallie was not burdened by the day-to-day responsibilities of the trip; she was therefore free to explore a new and exciting landscape and described her experiences with a refreshing, youthful enthusiasm. "We made our way to the very edge of the cliff and looked down. We could hear the water dashing, splashing and roaring as if angry at the small space through which it was forced to pass. We were gone so long that the train was stopped and men sent out in search of us. We made all sorts of promises to remain in sight in the future."

Sallie Hester made the trip west with brothers William and John, younger sister Lottie, and parents Martha and Craven. Her diary first appeared in seven serialized episodes in *The Argonaut*, a California weekly periodical, from September 1 through October 24, 1925. The entire diary covers the years 1849 to 1871, beginning with her family's departure for California and ending with her marriage in 1871. Only that portion of the diary describing her overland experience is published here.

Sallie's final journal entry describes her marriage to James K. Maddock on October 5, 1871 and with it ends our association with Sallie Hester:

> I was married to James K. Maddock of Eureka, Nevada. A quiet wedding, only a few intimate friends present. . . . Refreshments were served and we left soon after for Eureka. Spent a few days in Sacramento . . . I am once more a stranger in a strange land, and now, Dear Journal, I give thee up. No more jottings down of gay and festive scenes—the past is gone and the future is before me. "So mote it be."

ဿ *The Diary of a Pioneer Girl by Sallie Hester* ရ

Bloomington, Indiana, Tuesday, March 20, 1849.—Our family, consisting of father, mother, two brothers and one sister, left this morning for that far and much talked of country, California. My father started our wagons one month in advance, to St. Joseph, Missouri, our starting point. We take the steamboat to New Albany, going by water to St. Joe. The train leaving Bloomington on that memorable occasion was called the Missionary Train, from the fact that the Rev. Isaac Owens of the Methodist Church and a number of ministers of the same denomination were sent as missionaries to California. Our train numbered fifty wagons.

The last hours were spent in bidding good bye to old friends. My mother is heartbroken over the separation of relatives and friends. Giving up old associations for what? Good health, perhaps? My father is going in search of health, not gold. The last goodbye has been said—the last glimpse of our old home on the hill and wave of the hand at the old Academy, with a good bye to kind teachers and schoolmates, and we are off. We have been several days reaching New Albany [Indiana] on account of the terrible condition of the roads. Our carriage upset at one place. All were thrown out, but no one was hurt. We were detained several hours on account of this accident. My mother thought it a bad omen and wanted to return and give up the trip.

ဿရ

New Albany, March 24.   This is my first experience of a big city and my first glimpse of a river and steamboats.

ဿရ

March 26.   Took the steamboat *Meteor* this evening for St. Joe Now sailing on the broad Ohio, floating toward the far West.

ဿရ

St. Louis, April 2.   Spent the day here, enjoyed everything.

ဿရ

Reprinted from *Covered wagon women: Diaries and letters from the western trails, 1840–1849*, vol. 1, edited and compiled by Kenneth L. Holmes by permission of the University of Nebraska Press. © 1983 by Kenneth L. Holmes.

April 3.   On the Missouri River, the worst in the world, sticking on sand bars most of the time.

Jefferson City, April 6.   Stopped here for one hour, visited the State House, enjoyed everything.

K∽Cᴙ

April 14.   Our boat struck another sand bar and was obliged to land passengers ten miles below St. Joe. Having our carriage with us, we were more fortunate than others. We reached the first day an old log hut, five miles from town, where we camped for the night. Next day an old friend of my father heard of our arrival, came to see us and insisted that we stay at his home until we hear from our wagons.

K∽Cᴙ

FIGURE 5.1   Covered wagons pulled by oxen. The photograph was taken 1870–1880. (Western History Collection/Genealogy Department, Denver Public Library, X-21874)

St. Joe, April 27.   Here we are at last, safe and sound. We expect to remain here several days, laying in supplies for the trip and waiting our turn to be ferried across the river. As far as eye can reach, so great is the emigration, you see nothing but wagons. This town presents a striking appearance—a vast army on wheels—crowds of men, women and lots of children and last but not least the cattle and horses upon which our lives depend.

℘)ℛ

May 1 [Sunday].   Crossed the river. Camped six miles from town. Remained here several days, getting things shipshape for our long trip.

℘)ℛ

May 13 [Sunday].   This is a small Indian village. There is a mission at this place, about thirty pupils, converts to the Christian faith. Left camp May 6, and have been travelling all week. We make it a point to rest over Sunday. Have a sermon in camp every Sunday morning and evening. I take advantage of this stopover to jot down our wanderings during the week.

℘)ℛ

May 21 Sunday.   Camped on the beautiful Blue River, 215 miles from St. Joe, with plenty of wood and water and good grazing for our cattle. Our family all in good health. When we left St. Joe my mother had to be lifted in and out of our wagons; now she walks a mile or two without stopping, and gets in and out of the wagons as spry as a young girl. She is perfectly well. We had two deaths in our train within the past week of cholera—young men going West to seek their fortunes. We buried them on the banks of the Blue River, far from home and friends. This is a beautiful spot. The Plains are covered with flowers. We are now in the Pawnee Nation—a dangerous and hostile tribe. We are obliged to watch them closely and double our guards at night. They never make their appearance during the day, but skulk around at night, steal cattle and do all the mischief they can. When we camp at night, we form a corral with our wagons and pitch our tents on the outside, and inside of this corral we drive our cattle, with the guards stationed on the outside of tents. We have a cooking stove made of sheet iron, a portable table, tin plates and cups, cheap knives and forks (best ones packed away), camp stools, etc. We sleep in our wagons on feather beds; the men who drive for us in the tent. We live on bacon, ham, rice, dried fruits, molasses, packed butter, bread, coffee, tea and milk as we have our own cows. Occasionally some of the men kill an antelope and then we have a feast; and sometimes we have fish on Sunday.

ℬℭ

Fort Kearney, May 24.   This fort is built of adobe with walls of same.

ℬℭ

Sunday, June 3.   Our tent is now pitched on the beautiful Platte River, 315 miles from St. Joe. The cholera is raging. A great many deaths; graves everywhere. We as a company are all in good health. Game is scarce; a few antelope in sight. Roads bad.

ℬℭ

Goose Creek, June 17 [Sunday].   This is our day of rest. There are several encampments in sight, making one feel not quite out of civilization. So many thousands all en route for the land of gold and Italian skies! Passed this week Court House Rock. Twelve miles from the point is Chimney Rock, 230 feet in height.

ℬℭ

Fort Laramie, June 19.   This fort is of adobe, enclosed with a high wall of the same. The entrance is a hole in the wall just large enough for a person to crawl through. The impression you have on entering is that you are in a small town. Men were engaged in all kinds of business from blacksmith up. We stayed here some time looking at everything that was to be seen and enjoying it to the fullest extent after our long tramp. We camped one mile from the fort, where we remained a few days to wash and lighten up.

ℬℭ

June 21.   Left camp and started over the Black Hills, sixty miles over the worst road in the world. Have again struck the Platte and followed it until we came to the ferry. Here we had a great deal of trouble swimming our cattle across, taking our wagons to pieces, unloading and replacing our traps. A number of accidents happened here. A lady and four children were drowned through the carelessness of those in charge of the ferry.

ℬℭ

Bear River, July 1 [Sunday].   Lots of Indians in sight, mostly naked, disgusting and dirty looking.

FIGURE 5.2 Independence Rock, Wyoming. Noted landmark on the Oregon Trail, a granite dome rising out of the Sweetwater Plain, 195 feet high and 1,500 yards in circumference. Sallie carved her name on the rock like thousands of overland travelers. (ARC Identifier 516895, Variant Control Number NWDNS-57-HS-286, National Archives and Records Administration, College Park, MD)

ဢၢ

July 2.   Passed Independence Rock. This rock is covered with names. With great difficulty I found a place to cut mine. Twelve miles from this is Devil's Gate. It's an opening in the mountain through which the Sweetwater River flows. Several of us climbed this mountain—somewhat perilous for young-sters not over fourteen. We made our way to the very edge of the cliff and looked down. We could hear the water dashing, splashing and roaring as if angry at the small space through which it was forced to pass. We were gone so long that the train was stopped and men sent out in search of us. We made all sorts of promises to remain in sight in the future. John Owens, a son of the minister, my brother John, sister Lottie and myself were the quartet. During the week we passed the South Pass and the summit of the Rocky Mountains. Four miles from here are the Pacific Springs.

ॐ

Lee Springs, July 4 [Wednesday].   Had the pleasure of eating ice. At this point saw lots of dead cattle left by the emigrants to starve and die. Took a cutoff; had neither wood nor water for fifty-two miles. Traveled in the night. Arrived at Green River next day at two o'clock in the afternoon. Lay by two days to rest man and beast after our long and weary journey.

ॐ

July 29 [Sunday].   Passed Soda Springs. Two miles further on are the Steamboat Springs. They puff and blow and throw water high in the air. The springs are in the midst of a grove of trees, a beautiful and romantic spot.

ॐ

August 3.   Took another cutoff this week called Sublets. Struck Raft River; from thence to Swamp Creek. Passed some beautiful scenery, high cliffs of rocks resembling old ruins or dilapidated buildings.

ॐ

Hot Springs, August 18.   Camped on a branch of Mary's River, a very disagreeable and unpleasant place on account of the water being so hot. This week some of our company left us, all young men. They were jolly, merry fellows and gave life to our lonely evenings. We all miss them very much. Some had violins, others guitars, and some had fine voices, and they always had a good audience. They were anxious to hurry on without the Sunday stops. Roads are rocky and trying to our wagons, and the dust is horrible. The men wear veils tied over their hats as a protection. When we reach camp at night they are covered with dust from head to heels.

ॐ

Humboldt River, August 20.   We are now 348 miles from the mines. We expect to travel that distance in three weeks and a half. Water and grass scarce.

ॐ

St. Mary's River, August 25.   Still traveling down the Humboldt. Grass has been scarce until today. Though the water is not fit to drink—slough water— we are obliged to use it, for it's all we have.

℘ℂℛ

St. Mary's, September 2 [Sunday].   After coming through a dreary region of country for two or three days, we arrived Saturday night. We had good grass but the water was bad. Remained over Sunday. Had preaching in camp.

℘ℂℛ

September 4.   Left the place where we camped last Sunday. Traveled six miles. Stopped and cut grass for cattle and supplied ourselves with water for the desert. Had a trying time crossing. Several of our cattle gave out, and we left one. Our journey through the desert was from Monday, three o'clock in the afternoon, until Thursday morning at sunrise, September 6. The weary journey last night, the mooing of the cattle for water, their exhausted condition, with the cry of "Another ox down," the stopping of train to unyoke the poor dying brute, to let him follow at will or stop by the wayside and die, and the weary, weary tramp of men and beasts, worn out with heat and famished for water, will never be erased from my memory. Just at dawn, in the distance, we had a glimpse of Truckee River, and with it the feeling: Saved at last! Poor cattle; they kept on mooing, even when they stood knee deep in water. The long dreaded desert has been crossed and we are all safe and well. Here we rested Thursday and Friday—grass green and beautiful, and the cattle are up to their eyes in it.

℘ℂℛ

September 8.   Traveled fourteen miles; crossed Truckee twelve times.

℘ℂℛ

September 9.   Sunday, our day of rest.

℘ℂℛ

Monday, September 10.   Traveled four miles down to the end of the valley.

℘ℂℛ

Tuesday, September 11.   Made eighteen miles. Crossed Truckee River ten times. Came near being drowned at one of the crossings. Got frightened and jumped out of the carriage into the water. The current was very swift and carried me some distance down the stream.

℘)℘

Thursday, September 14.   We arrived at the place where the Donner Party perished, having lost their way and being snowed in. Most of them suffered and died from want of food. This was in 1846. Two log cabins, bones of human beings and animals, tops of the trees being cut off the depth of the snow, was all that was left to tell the tale of that ill-fated party, their sufferings and sorrow. A few of their number made their way out, and after days of agony and hunger finally reached Sutter's Fort. We crossed the summit of the Sierra Nevada. It was night when we reached the top, and never shall I forget our descent to the place where we are now encamped—our tedious march with pine knots blazing in the darkness and the tall, majestic pines towering above our heads. The scene was grand and gloomy beyond description. We could not ride—roads too narrow and rocky—so we trudged along, keeping pace with the wagons as best we could. This is another picture engraven upon the tablets of memory. It was a footsore and weary crowd that reached that night our present camping place.

℘)℘

Yuba Valley, Sunday, September 16.   We are now 108 miles from Sutter's Fort.

℘)℘

September 17.   Left camp this morning. Traveled down the lower end of the valley. Lay by two days. Had a preaching out under the pines at night. The men built a fire and we all gathered around it in camp-meeting style.

℘)℘

September 19.   Started once more. Roads bad, almost impassable. After traveling for twenty-five miles we halted for one day. Good grass three miles from camp.

℘)℘

September 21.   Reached Bear Valley by descending a tremendous hill. We let the wagons down with ropes. Stopped over Sunday. At Sleepy Hollow we

FIGURE 5.3 Weary pioneers rest in front of two Conestoga wagons on a plain with mountains in the background, around 1870. (Western History/Genealogy Department, Denver Public Library, X-11929)

again let our wagons down the mountain with ropes. Rested in the hollow, ate our dinner and then commenced our weary march over the mountain. Left one of our wagons and the springs of our carriage. Cut down trees for our cattle to browse on. Thanks to a kind Providence we are nearing the end of our long and perilous journey. Came on to Grass Valley and rested four or five days.

᯽

October 1 [Monday].   Arrived at Johnson's Fort. Thence we went to Nicholson's ranch.

᯽

Vernon, California, October 6.   Well, after a five month's trip from St. Joe, Missouri, our party of fifty wagons, now only thirteen, has at last reached this haven of rest. Strangers in a strange land—what will the future be? This town is situated at the junction of the Feather and Sacramento rivers.

In the Classroom_____

Chronological Thinking

- Create a time line of the major events contained in Sallie's diary.
- Cite specific diary entries to show change in Sallie's attitude toward the overland crossing over the course of her journey.

Historical Comprehension

- Write a letter from Sallie's perspective to a schoolmate back in Indiana describing the overland crossing.
- Trace Sallie's route on a physical map of the United States identifying the geographical obstacles she and her family had to overcome.

Historical Analysis and Interpretation

- Analyze whether the history of the United States would have changed, if at all, had gold not been discovered in California.
- Describe how Sallie is similar and different from young girls today.

Historical Research Capabilities

- Potential Topics:
  Oregon Trail   Sutter's Mill
  St. Joseph, Missouri Independence Rock
  Donner Party

Historical Issues-Analysis and Decision-Making

- Identify the three major reasons people made the overland crossing west to Oregon and California.
- Analyze the impact of the overland migration on the indigenous people with whom the emigrants came into contact.

6

Civil War: The Diary of Charles Whipple Hadley

"Had my picture taken without & with uniform." Seventeen-year-old Charles Whipple Hadley proudly posed in his new Corporal's uniform on November 20, 1861. He placed his left hand inside his tunic and tried to remain motionless for the photographer. On March 25, 1863, Hadley again posed for a photograph, his physique somewhat sturdier and whiskers certainly more impressive. His eyes, however, present the greatest contrast between the two photographs and reflect what this young man witnessed and experienced in the intervening sixteen months.

After the fall of Fort Sumter, President Lincoln called for the states to raise 75,000 volunteers to end the uprising. The Union required recruits to be at least eighteen years of age, but thousands of young men like Charles Whipple Hadley managed to enlist. Hadley joined the 14th Regiment of Iowa Volunteer Infantry in the fall of 1861, thirsting for adventure and eager to serve his country in a time of great need. The adventure would have to wait, however, for first a soldier's business had to be learned and that meant drill and more drill. "Today has been a busy day drill has been principal business." "Today is the coldest day we have had since we left Camp McClellan but it has not prevented us from drilling." "[W]e drilled for an hour without stopping, the hardest drill we have had." Hadley was particularly proud of his prowess with a rifle. "I was third best shot the first hitting the paper, 4 inches square."

The drill, the endless marches and, most exasperating, the waiting in camp proved tedious and boring. Hadley and his fellow volunteers spent considerable time and energy trying to combat the less

FIGURE 6.1   Charles Whipple Hadley. The photograph on the left was taken on November 20, 1861, the one on the right on March 25, 1863. (L. Tom Perry Special Collections, Harold B. Lee Library, Brigham Young University, MSS 177)

romantic side of a soldier's life. "Crame Eaton & two others are playing seven up for the apples by my side I am considered in of course." "They are having a dance over here in the cabin." "I have just returned form a debating meetings." "[T]he boys pass the time away playing ball checkers marbles & laying in the shade."

The tedium and boredom abruptly ended on February 12, 1862 when the 14th Iowa Regiment, now part of General Ulysses S. Grant's Army of the Tennessee, laid siege to Confederate-held Fort Donelson in Tennessee. "O'Neil just shot in head Sargent a few feet from me just shot. Sveral Color Guards killed Seales & I all right yet. Its tough but that is what we enlisted for." Less than two months after the Union victory at Fort Donelson, Hadley participated in one of the bloodiest battles in American history.

Though referred to in Hadley's diary as Pittsburgh Landing, the battle is best known and remembered as the Battle of Shiloh. "[T]he report came in that our pickets have been driven in & rebels are advancing to the attack we are ready for them." One hundred thousand men took part in the battle on April 6–7, with twenty-five thousand killed, wounded, or captured. Hadley was among the latter. "[W]e commenced falling back as the enemy came up . . . we lost many we drew up at the camp of the 3d Iowa here we were entirely surrounded & had to surrender . . . I am sound as a brick but had some close calls."

Early in the war, captured troops were exchanged right on the field of battle: a private for a private, a sergeant for a sergeant, a colonel for a colonel, and so on. "[W]here we are going is a mistery to all, the quarter master said that we were to be exchanged." As the war progressed and the number of captives soared, a parole system was established. Prisoners vowed not to take up arms against their captors until they could be formally exchanged for an opponent of equal rank. "Saturday afternoon a paper was circulated to get the names of those who were willing to take the oath & go home, if that was the only way, about 600 signed the list."

While details of the parole were being arranged, Hadley and his fellow prisoners were transported all around the South. Treatment was occasionally harsh. "We have been four days & nights in a freight car there was 46 of us in one car. None of us could sleep. . . . we are all completly worn out." Unlike most Union prisoners in the South, however, Hadley felt lucky. "We were marched to this place which is an old Fair, & now goes by the name of Camp Oglethrope . . . with guards stationed around the out side, it is a splendid place here we shall enjoy our selves."

"After two months stay in Southern prisons are set at liberty by parole which is our view prohibits us from any Military duty whatsoever." Hadley and his fellow prisoners were officially paroled in June 1862. Ironically, he returned to Benton Barracks where his journey had begun the previous November. "Here we are again after the lapse of six months during which time we have seen & experienced soldiers life in all it forms & privations."

Charles Whipple Hadley was born on February 11, 1844. He was discharged as a Sergeant on March 25, 1863. He died at Ogden City, Utah on July 20, 1936 at the age of 92. On the inside front cover of his diary is a little poem in the author's handwriting:

> Steal not this book
> For Fear of shame
> For just above
> You find my name
>
> C. W. H.

℘ *The Diary of C. W. Hadley* ℘

JOURNAL BY C. W. HADLEY
DURING THE WAR 1861–2
ANAMOSA, IOWA

In Oct. E. L. Warner raised a company of men for the three years Service. I enlisted on Oct 12th 1861. We started for Davenport shortly after on the 6th of Nov. we were joined by part of a company enlisted by Buell & Cawkins. We were sworn into the U.S. Service the same day. . . .

I am 2d Corporal Co H 14th Iowa Pay $13.00 per month

℘)℘

Nov 20th 1861

Had my picture taken without & with uniform

℘)℘

5 O'clock A.M.
Jollyett Ill. Nov 29th 1861

We started from Davenport about dusk, & travelled all night we reached this place at about four Oclock this morning & we start down the Ill. Central in about one hour. four Co's are here all half starved to death we cannot get anything to eat in town.

C. W. Hadley

℘)℘

Benton Barracks Mo.
St. Louis Nov. 30th 1861

From Jolyett we took the Ill. Cen. R R & reached the city of Flton about 12 Oclock at night, we went immediately to the Steamboat "Meteor" on board of which we stayed all night, starting at 6 in the morning we reached St. Louis about 8 Oclock A.M. distance 25 M. after about two hr delay we reached Benton Barraks, situated in the suburbs of the city about five miles from the landing. The grounds take up about a mile sq. the ground is perfectly levell & dry.

Hadley, Charles Whipple, *Diary and correspondence, 1861–1913*, MSS 177, L. Tom Perry Special Collections, Harold B. Lee Library, Brigham Young University.

The 12th Iowa Reg. arrived here to-night. There are now about 18,000 (30,000) men now in camp the camp ground includes the Fair Ground the 9th Reg's concentrate about 60,000 men here for a grand movement.

C. W. Hadley

ဆၢဢ

Benton Barracks St. Louis Dec 3

Yesterday we had our first drill by Co. today first drill by Battallion since we came to Benton. B. Last night a man was shot while on guard duty day before yesterday a man was shot trying to run the guard. My candle is going out or I would write more

C. W. Hadley

ဆၢဢ

Camp Benton St. Louis Dec 6th 1861

All has gone well as far as know in camp. I got a pass this morning from the Col. signed at Head Quarters and went to town (St. Louis). I took the cars (horse) at the entrance and started about 2 Oclock A.M. It is about 3 M. to town from Camp. After getting there I did not know where to go, so I strolled around here & there determined to see the sights you can go one block and see it all it's all alike. I got a dish of Oisters for dinner (.25). at a Saloon I also bought a flute (1.50) & book (.50) I have not received a single letter from home by mail I have recd. 3 or 4 by private conveyance. . . .

Dr. Chapman came down the other day he was appointed a place in the quartermater department. The tattoo is beating I must retire (go to bed).

C. W. Hadley

ဆၢဢ

Camp Benton St. Louis Dec 9th

I am quite sick this morning I was taken with a very severe sick headache yesterday about noon and kept growing worse untill near night the doctor told me that I had a feaver. this morning I feel better my head does not ache as bad, yet my back aches very bad. I have very little feaver this morning our barrack is being remodelled today I am for the present in the officers quarters in the upper bunk lying on my back writing this

C. W. Hadley

໒໑

Benton Barracks Dec. 12 1861

Today I took part in the morning drill. But Delaplain 2d Sar. put us on double quick & kept it up so long that being quite weak I come most going out I did not dare to try it in the 10 Oclock drill I went in the Battallion drill. I took a fellow to the guard House today to stay untill tomorrow. today while we were on drill we saw a couple of buildings on fire just out side the guard lines on returning we enquired about it & was told that last night some Sharp Shooters went over there & one of them having some misunderstanding with an Old Man who kept it the son took it up for his father & nearly stabed him to death on the ground (he has died since) the Soldiers went over the morning burnt the Grocery & House took the man wife and son prisoners a sesession flag was found in the House. . . .

C. W. Hadley

໒໑

Guard House Western Div. of Guard Line
Benton Barracks St. Louis Dec 15 1861 8 O'clock A.M.

Yesterday I went on duty as corporal of the guard at 8 O'clock yesterday I have only seven men on my relief last night was the most interesting night of all. The Officer of the guard of our Division gave orders not to allow any soldiers to pass along the road running along our beats. right after sundown soldiers began to pass along, as fast as they came along we would halt them & if they had the counter sign we let them pass, if not we held them subject to the order of the Officer if the guard some of them would not stop untill they heard the click of our guns lock's then their courage failed them & they come too, on some we found whiskey others were going after it. When they found they were caught they would beg hard to be let go but in vain. We caught two who told us that the guard No. 4 let them out. He was immediately arrested & put in the Guard House & He will be court Martialed he had let out 15 others He will likely be sent up for 6 month ball & chain But here comes the new guard I must close

C. W. Hadley

໒໑

Camp Benton Mon. 16th Dec.

Today has been a busy day drill has been the principal business. Tonight I received a letter from Home one from Mother & One from father & Elegene they are all well, it is court week, my father says he is very busy. It is nearly time to get to bed I must close

C. W. Hadley

જીલ્લ

Camp Benton. Dec. 18th 9 O'clock

Nothing unusual has occured this morning. Our news this morning was that New Orleans was taken & that we had whiped them twice in Kentucky. I am excused from drill this morning the Co. is out. I answered my fathers letter yesterday

જીલ્લ

Benton Barracks. Dec. 20

Today is the coldest day we have had since we left Camp McClellan but it has not prevented us from drilling. This morning after dinner we started on a double quick for the Infantry drill ground about three quarters of a mile from our Barrack and we kept it up for nearly a mile, then taking the quick step we drilled for an hour without stopping, the hardest drill we have had. We got the news today that we had taken 1300 men two ton of powder 1,000 horses etc.

I had a sick headach this afternoon & got excused from R drill & D parade. Crame Eaton & two others are playing seven up for the apples by my side I am considered in of course   Carr Hall is getting over the Measles, & the 1st Lieut. (Cawkins) is quite sick no better tonight.

C. W. Hadley

જીલ્લ

Benton Barracks Dec 25th

Today is Christmass as usual on the 25th of Dec We have not drilled today excepting a few minutes this morning. It has been quite wet the snow has almost melted I heard today my best girl was dead. The Tatoos is trying to beat I must quit.

C. W. Hadley

જીલ્લ

FIGURE 6.2 Civil War recruiting poster. (Collection of the New York Historical Society, PR-055-3-221)

Benton Barracks Dec. 27

This morning it was quite cold, we had a short drill. My arm which was vacinated is extremely painful   17th Iowa recd. guns   It makes one about half sick, our boy in the hospatl are getting better, we expect our guns today.

ஐௐ

Benton Barracks Dec 28th

Our guns came today but upon trial were found to be of a poor quality & the Captains refused to receipt for them. We borrowed thirty more guns making 45 in all to drill with untill we get ours the 3D Iowa Infentry & the 55 Ill has left the Barracks within the last week the 12th I got their guns today

C W H

ဆာလ

7½ Oclock P, M
Benton Barracks Dec 30 <u>Guns bursted</u>

Since noon I have been quite sick. I do not know what ails me. today the Cap & 45 men from different Companies took some more of those muskets & tried them out of 45, 14 busted　　They were pill lock Russion muskets & we marched to Headquarters & throwed them over the fence.

C. W. Hadley

ဆာလ

Jan. 1st—1862
Benton Barracks Jan 1st 1862

Today is the dawning of a new year one that no doubt will prove an eventful one, the camp has been all excitement. It was expected that an attempt would be made to release the prisoners in the city membering about 5,000–800 cavalry men were ordered to mount in twenty minutes, an order then came for them to stand by their horses armed & equiped untill fartherward came this morning one company was ordered to the city in haste. all the armed regiments were order to be ready at a moments warning.

　　This morning Mrs & Mr Smith the Leuts. & myself drank to the perpituity of the Union　　tonight we are having a general good time in the kitchen. I wrote home today

C. W. Hadley

ဆာလ

BENTON Barracks St. Louis Jan 9

Fred Haymaker died this morning at three OClock he did not have his senses when dying. his body is to be sent home

　　It is very foggy & muddy today I have just mailed a letter for home I was expected on the sick list this morning I have been on for the last week. I have a very large boil on my face just under the left corner of my mouth it is very painful Jas Eaton was here a few minutes ago he just came out of the Hospital. Hubbard & Case were taken with the measles yesterday. We had no Brigade drill this afternoon

C. W. Hadley

⧉

Recd Guns
Benton Barracks St. Louis Jan 11

Today the weather is quite pleasant although cold yesterday we got our guns the same that they have been trying to have us take for so long. We tried them today at 125 yards I was third best shot the first hitting the paper, 4 inches square. the Major says we are under marching orders.

C. W. Hadley

⧉

Feb 5th P.M. 1862
Steamboat Express between Jefferson Barracks. S. W.

We started this morning about 7 Oclock from the Barracks, reached the boat in about two hrs. yet we did not get started untill afternoon. We are bound for Corie we received orders night before last to be ready to march in twenty four hours. the passage so far has been quite pleasant The weather has been quite warm. I wrote home yesterday (last night) telling them where we were going

⧉

Paudaca Kentucky Feb. 7

We arrived at Cario about noon today & then learned the Fort Henry Tenn. had been taken by our gunboats two of which were at Cario one of the boats had been hit in the . . . which caused it to burst scalding 20 men the boat was left at the Fort. Their loses in not known we received orders to proceed up the Ohio R. & Tenn. R. & Jamestown the fort I expect we will lay over here tonight we met here the 14th Ohio Battery bound for Fort Leavenworth, They are having a dance over here in the cabin. today we tried our guns they are a good thing.

C. W. H.

⧉

Fort Henry Tennessee Feb. 8th

We arrived here about Ten Oclock the rebells left here day before yesterday we took about 100 prisoners we pitched our tents & will camp here tonight

C. W. H.

ℰꝆ

Fort Henry Tennessee Feb 11th 1862
On Tennessee River

We are Still at Fort Henry But tomorrow we leave for the naborhood of Fort Donalson twelve miles west of here two Brigades have already gone. We belong to the forth brigade. we have orders to march at eight O'clock in the evening. Birds Sharp shooters belong to our brigade. the 2nd Brigade leaves tomorrow at 4 A.M.

There are 50,000 men now in this camp & 40,000 within six miles of here.

C. W. Hadley

ℰꝆ

Sun rise Feb 13th—62
Tennessee two miles from Fort Donalson on the Cumberland.

We started from For Henry at about 10 Oclock yesterday morning we reached here about dusk travelling about 12 miles We are about two miles from For Donalson last night we were marched about half mile in the woods from the road we then laid down wrapte in our blankets. We were not allowed any fire until about an hour ago We passed a very pleasant night for we were all so near tired out that we nearly all slept sound as bricks some 8 shots (Cannon) have already been fired in the direction of the Fort. Today we expect to see some fight ing we have in the ranks sicty men exclusive, of the Sargent & Commissioned Officers.

C. W. Hadley

ℰꝆ

About 5 P.M. were in a pit & can't go ahead or get out. Im within 6 rods of the works O'Neil just shot in head Sargent a few feet from me just shot. Several Color Guards killed   Seales & I all right yet. Its tough but that is what we enlisted for

C W H

ℰꝆ

Fort Donaldson Tenn. Feb 17th, Monday eve 10 P.M.

We now ocapy the inner fort. Scarcely had I finished my last entry, before we were ordered into line. Steping to our places as our guns were stacked & taking arms, we were marched in front in Brigade line of battle   we proceeded in line through brush & over fallen trees for half mile when to our astonishment we came within good Musket range of the works only seperated by a deep ravine we were greeted with a few balls, here we halted & formed, well imagining what we met. one could see our skirmushers at work below. Soon the order was given to forward, & down the hill we went without any body's being hurt, but on started up the hill on the top of which was the works, we received a storm of bullets. 8 of Co. H were wounded at the first fire. Nealy was cut across the temple & with the exclamation Oh Murder I'm shot he rolled over & was taken off. Gowen recd. a ball on the big toe & over he went, one was shot through the hand another through the wrist, which will keep him from duty as long a posible. Orderly Burk recd. a hole through the hat, no one was killed one of the color guards of which I am one was shot through the head within two feet of me spattering the blood on my left arm and face. I had a bullet go through my cartridge box and a bullet struck inside my belt & go around a buckle hole & came through nearly cutting one in two as it seemed.

Corp. Hall one of our guards, was shot through the head by my side the blood spurted on to my left arm & face I recd. a shot through the cartridge box and one when we came to withing thirty or forty yds. of the work we were ordered to tree this we did in short order Co. H all laid down in a little hollow I soon left there and run up the hill & got behind a stump & got six or eight good shots at the rebels, we laid under heavy fire of ball & shell for 7 hours till dark we then fell back to the hollow marched onto the hill & laid on our arms all night during two hrs. rain then it snowed & froze. We all nearly froze to death next morning we camped on the ground. when were in brigade line of battle the 12th Iowa was on our rith the 25th India. & 7 Iowa on our left, in this order we charged the works.

Friday we stood by our arms all day, at night I had a severe attack of the rheumatism & went to the hospital at five next morning I joined the reg. Saturdya morning we were kept in line of battle, about noon a mesenger came dashing down to the Col. he ordered us to arms we were marched in four ranks by the left flank for half mile to an open field here we were in full view of the brest works we saw the works were being stormed we were ordered to storm in line of battle we went up the hill at a double quick untill we had passed the brest works we were then ordered to lie low, we laid here for half an hour under a terrible fire we were then ordered behind the works we fell back in good order, the Iowa 2d were the first to cross the works this they did nobly with the bayonet only, the 14th charged through the Sally port, after the enemy were driven behind their 2d works, the 2d, 14th & others fell back to the outer works. Here the 2d, 14th & others laid on their arms all night Next morning they prepared to storm the 2d works when the white flag was seen on their works they were given half an hour to surrender in this they did. the troops then marched in by Regiments the Iowa 2d taking the lead. We are now camped in their log huts in the main fort. the men taken were about 17000 man our order was read from Gen Grant commanding our Bregade for making the first landing on the works & holding till surrender

৪১৫২

Fort Donalson Feb 20th Wed.

. . . It is rumored that we are under marching orders for Nashville to take that place, the rebels are expected to make a stand there. I wrote to my Folks last night. I have not recd. a letter from them since I left St. Louis

C. W. Hadley

৪১৫২

Fort Donalson Tenn. Sun. Feb 23d 1862

We are still here at this Fort & do not know when we are to leave we heard tonight that Nashville had been evacuated by the rebels we expected to participate in the taking of that place, but were glad to hear of its evacuation . . .

৪১৫২

Camp McClernard 4 Ms. above Ft. Foot March 11th

We left For Donalson on the 7th the first night we camped about three miles from here on a creek, and reached here about 10 Oclock next morning we are now camped at the mouth of a ravine about 1½ ms. from the Tenn. River . . .

৪১৫২

Camp McClernard or landing Mar. 12th

We are still here we expect to go today yet it is uncertain when it has been rumered here for sometime that Mannassa was taken it is only a rumer though.

৪১৫২

March 15 7½ P.M. McClernard's landing on board steam boat

Today it has rained all day & of course it is just the luck that the 14th Reg. should leave in the mud we made out to get here though through the rain most of us wet through. we are on first deck back end . . .

C. W. Hadley

ৡৈৰ

March 21st Pitsburg 13 ms. above Savanah Tenn.

We started from McClernards landing Mar. 11th we left Savanah the morning of the 18th we reached here that night. We pitched tents about a mile from the river day before yesterday the rebels are about 20 ms. from here.

C. W. H.

FIGURE 6.3 Photograph of camp scene taken by famed Civil war photographer Matthew Brady. (ARC Identifier 524637, Variant Control Number NWDNS-111-B-218, National Archives and Records Administration, College Park, MD)

ℰↃℭℛ

Pitsburg Landing Sat. Mar. 2d

We are still here, rumor say we are to go forward in four days. It is reported that the quarter master read in a St. Louis paper that Island No. 10 Miss. R. was taken with Beaureguard & 14,000 Prisoners The Iowas Boys were much cut up at Cross Roads Ark's In the 9th Iowa no acquaintance but C. Marcellus was wounded, & one young & Cap Drips killed . . .

C. W. Hadley

ℰↃℭℛ

Pitsburg Landing Tenn. Mar 31st

There is little to write deserters from the rebels report 80,000 at Corinth 20 miles from here   Island No. 10 not yet taken   troops are still coming in to camp   the river has fallen about 20 feet since we came here.
     Co. K burried a Maj. yesterday No late news from home all quite on the Potomac

C. W. Hadley

ℰↃℭℛ

9½ P.M.
Pitsburg Landing Apr. 4th

We are still here yet with two days rations in our sacks ready to march at a moments warning. the report came in that our pickets have been driven in & rebels are advancing to the attack we are ready for them. Sargent Delaplain returned to duty tonight he was left sick at St. Louis the 16th Iowa arrived tonight Leut Fuller was up here.

C. W. Hadley

ℰↃℭℛ

9 P.M. Friday
Pitsburg Landing Apr. 5th 1862

We are still here, the alarm of last night has died away the Iowa 6th took 9 or ten rebels they took 3 or 4 of our boys it seems that they were making a reconnoiance in force Buell is reported at Florence all is quite.

C. W. Hadley

℘℩℘

Centre Hill Tenn. Apri. Mon. 7

The place we were marched to after being captured, camped on a corn field & laid in mud rained all night. Yesterday the rebels commenced the attack upon our lines they fell back upon the main body then the fight became general our bregade was brought into axtion about 9 O'clock A.M. we sustained two charges & drove them back with heavy loss they left their dead & wounded on the field. We laid on the ground gained until about 9 O'clock when the enemy gained ground rapidly on our left flank we commenced falling back as the enemy came up the 14th Iowa covered the retreat about face & held them at bay for 15 minutes amid a perfect storm of ball & shell the 14 suffered terribly seeing that we were nearly cut off we fell back rapidly in the retreat we lost many we drew up at the camp of the 3d Iowa here we were entirely surrounded & had to surrender numbering according to the report made this morning 1,635, not quite 200 of the 14th Co. H. had 26 men taken 12 or 15 missing. . . . I am sound as a brick but had some close calls. I tried to get away & was captured seperate at 6:05 P.M.

C. W. Hadley

℘℩℘

Memphis Tenn. Apr. Wed. 9th

Rolen a deserter from the rebels & joined our company was taken from us Cornith & shot by rebels. We were marched from Centre Hill, the morning of the 7th we reached Cornith that night (20 m) we were then loaded onto the cars fighting during a heavy rain storm, 12,00 more prisoners came in that night to Cornith, Palmer Underwood Muzzy were among them.

We reached this place last night about 9 P.M. We were marched to a large stone house on the river our present quarters we are all in a jam rumor says our troops are gaining ground Buell had arrived with his forces & it is rumored that Island No. 10 Is ours three of the rebell gun boats are in the view below us they are wood.

C. W. Hadley

℘℩℘

Memphis 9th Com. 7 O'c

We are still here part of the prisoners have been taken up town the report is that we are to be taken to Tuscalacy Alabama. . . . Our boys are all in good spirits, the wounded ones doing well . . .

C. W. Hadley

$\wp\infty$

Memphis Tenn. Apri. 13th 12th Sunday

Yesterday we were marched through Memphis to the R. R. bound for Jackson Miss we got to the suburbs & the train stoped the guards said that a colvert had been washed away the night before, & here we are still we expect to go out this morning there are 40 of us in each car & 16 cars, the floor of our car is covered with mud we get two hard crackers . . .

$\wp\infty$

Mobile Alabama, Wednesday Apr. 16th 1862

. . . We reached Jackson about noon, here we were delayed several hours on the account of a train of people there were anxious to see & speak to a Yankee. . . . We reached this place this morning about 2 A.M. we are confined in a large cotton ware house but in what part of the city we do not know we expect to be moved to Tuscalucy Alb. in a short time. We have been four days & nights in a freight car there was 46 of us in one car. None of us could sleep . . . we are all completly worn out.

C. W. Hadley

$\wp\infty$

Mobile Alb. Friday Apr. 18th

Today is the same as usual with us. We got a couple of bake spiders & two tine plates & knives & forks. Tonight they brought in some flour 2½ Sac. & 3 large sacks of Corn Meal. (so scales says) One of the guards said that we had attacked New Orleans, & that they had attacked us again at Corrnith.

$\wp\infty$

Mobile Sat. Apri. 19th 5 O'c P.M..

We have recd. orders to March the boys are riging up with 2 days rations. We do not know where we go . . .

C. W. Hadley

૭᱒C᱒

Cahaba Alab. Monday Apri. 21

. . . We are at present quartered in a large unfinished ware house situated on the bank. The ladies of the town sent in a beautiful supply of cornbread & meat. We shall long remembered our breakfast, for we were hungry as dogs the boys are all in good spirits . . .

૭᱒C᱒

Cahaba Alab. Apri 26th

I have just returned form a debating meeting just organized & held in a room intended for an office to the Ware house. The question discussed was this resolved that the pen exerts greater influence than the sword, the question was ably discussed, it was decided in favor of the Neg. The next question in Resolved that the fear of punishment is a greater incentive to action than the hope of reward, to be discussed next on Mon. at 2 O'clock . . .

૭᱒C᱒

Cahaba Alab. Thurs. May 1st 1862

Last night it rained all night. This morning we drew two more days rations making four days rations that we have on hand. We also recd. orders to cook them immediately preparitory to leaving for some place unknown to us . . .

૭᱒C᱒

15 miles from Montgomery, steam-boat Reindeer Aba. River May 2d

Our 3 days rations were all cooked last night, this morning we were routed out at 4 O'clock & stowed on board, there are 800 of us on the lower deck, yet it is not crowded much we have no guards below all above, this trip so far has been the most pleasant one we have had at the C.S.A. we have all our cooking utensels aboard, where we are going is a mistery to all, the quarter master said that we were to be exchanged, we will wait & see.

C. W. H.

ℬↃⳍ

Sunrise   Montgomery Aba. May Sat 3d 1862

We arruved at montgomery last night at Sundown. we passed Selma about 10 O'c we were landed & marched about a mile South east of the town to the ampatheater in the Fair ground. It is a old one no seats remain it is fast going. to ruin, it is of wood & white washed. . . . The weather is very pleasant this morning the air is cool & refreshing. It is a question of great doubt wheather we go to our lines or into Georgia. I am of the other opinion, we expect to leave this morning in the cars

Chas. Ha.

ℬↃⳍ

May 3d

. . . We were marched to this place which is an old Fair, & now goes by the name of Camp Oglethrope, it is a large level piece of ground half shaded by pine trees we are just turned loose in here with guards stationed around the out side, it is a splendid place here we shall enjoy our selves the ground is covered with sod for the present we are stowed away in the shade.

ℬↃⳍ

Macon, Georgia Mon. May 5th 1862

Since we came here we have enjoyed our-selves, we have plenty of room & to spare, the boys pass the time away playing ball checkers marbles & laying in the shade, talking of home, our prospects and those of the rebels . . .

ℬↃⳍ

Camp Oglethorpe Macon Geo. May 6th 3½ P.M.

This is one of the most pleasant days we have had the boys have all playing ball, last night & this morning I wound a ball & we have just had a good game of ball for the first time during our captivity   We have a splendid large play ground . . .

C. W. H.

⋙⋘

Macon Geo. Thurs. May 15 2½ P.M.

Yesterday & today I have been quite unwell, I feel better this afternoon. Yesterday two more companies of rebel troops come in without arms for guards. . . . last night a man of an ILL. reg. died at the well, it was caused by eating onions on a weak stomache five corpses are awaiting burial, no Iowa boys have died. . . . I have just returned from the funeral services of five of the men not yet burried . . . deaths are quite frequent now. It is hoped that we will get out of this soon for a great many are sick.

⋙⋘

Macon Geo. Friday May 16th Sunset.

. . . Four prisoners have died at the hospital since yesterday noon, others are dangerously sick. I feel a little better today although weak, the weather is pleasant, our rations of bread have been cut short 500lbs, out of 1200 for three days.

C. W. Hadley

⋙⋘

Macon Geo. Mon May 19th

For the last two days I have neglected to make any entry. Saturday afternoon a paper was circulated to get the names of those who were willing to take the oath & go home, if that was the only way, about 600 signed the list, this they rebel major was to take to Savanah & present to the authorities & try & get our release on those terms, but major Hardee having to rejoin his regiment recomended it to the rebel major who takes command now. he promised to write thinking it necessity to send the names, we await the result. A man in Co. I. died this morning. They weather continues pleasant, the health of the camp is better, todays paper states all quiet at Corinth & Richmond 1000's of troops have passed yesterday & today

C. W. Hadley

⋙⋘

Camp Oglethorp Macon Geo. May 20th Tuesday

This morning we were formed in line of battle, as it was said that the major wished to give some inspections, he took his place in front of the lines, took a piece of paper from his pocket read a dispatch from Gen. Beauriguard dated Montgomery "May 19th 1862". The substance of it was that Gen. Beauriguard has ishued an order ordering all Sheloh prisoners . . . to be paroled . . . they are now taking the higth name, age color of hair & eyes in the group they will be able to get off by the last of the week . . .

∞⌘

Macon Georgia Thursday May 22d.

The boys are still here it is thought that they will go tomorrow evening . . .
12 A.M.

. . . we started from Macon on saturday morning by dint of their practice I am along I was measured after the order to fall in had been given. . . . we reached Atlanta day before yesterday about 4 O'clock P.M. & laid over there until 7½ Ock. we traveled all night & reached Chattanoga about 7 A.M. there we stayed untill about ½ hour ago, when we started . . .

∞⌘

Camp Taylor Huntsville Ala. May 29 Thursday

. . . by the time we arrived at the station the cars were there, we were then handed over to Col _____ took the cars & reached Huntsville last night at dusk, we slept in the Court House & had plenty to eat. I commenced a letter home this morning, we are now with the 10 Ohio Reg for the present.

C. W. Hadley

∞⌘

Between Purlaski & Columbia 10 ms. from the latter. Tenn.
June 2d Monday 10 O'clock P.M.

. . . We marched with the train enrout for Columbia the first night we camped 17 ms. from Huntsville, as the wagons had each two bales of cotton on board we were obliged to walk excepting the sick give out it was a tough march for the boys, myself, included . . . tomorrow we shall take the cars to Columbia . . .

᥉ᏻᏻ

Nashville Tenn. Wed. June 5th 1862

. . . about 4 P.M. we took the cars for this place & reached here at dusk the bridges are all guarded. We slept that night in the depot, in the morning we were marched to the fair ground, where we are now the grounds are about two miles from the depot, they are not very extensive, on account of the rascality of 4 or 5 boys the whole of us are guarded we sleep in the building we are to get clothing here, the general impression is that we are to be discharged . . .

C. W. Had

᥉ᏻᏻ

Nashville, Tenn. June 6th 8 P.M. Friday

No use to try to write my ink is out and every body borrows & I cannot refuse . . .

C. W. Hadl

᥉ᏻᏻ

Nashville Tenn. June 10th Tuesday Fair ground camp
Yesterdays observations

I started from here yesterday about 8 O'clock, calculating to be gone all day. I took the same road that we came here the name of the St. I dod not know, it is well shaded & is one of the princapal streets arriving in the central part of the city a mile from camp. . . . the next place I visited of interest was the state Capitol about ¾ of a mile from the river situated upon a high eminence commanding a view of the city of surrounding country the view from her was indeed magnificent for miles. . . . decinding I roamed around among the hall untill reaching the library & it not being locked I entered, here I stayed for a couple of hours vareously ocupied & there being a table & ink at hand I took down my observations on the spot . . .

᥉ᏻᏻ

Nashville June 12 1862

. . . when I came back they were having a convention out by the Spring & I immediately repared thither a committee had just returned & reported the following petition to the Gen. Commanding the post (Gen Van Dorn). We the undersigned committee in behalf of the paroled prisoners at the Fair Ground, would respectfully ask your attention to our condition

After two months stay in Southern prisons are set at liberty by parole which is our view prohibits us from any Military duty whatsoever our present situation is exceedingly unfavorable to health as may be seen by the no. of sick we are entirely destitute of money to supply our many wants & necessities of our families many of which are suffering for want of the support usualy derived from us. Therefore in consideration of these facts we respectfully ask for transportation in order that we may report ourselves to our goveners in compliance with Orders 36 sec 4

C. W. Hadley, Carrier

ဆာ

Gallaton Ky June 30th 1862. 7 A.M.

We left Nashville this morning at five day before yesterday morning we recd. orders to draw two days rations & be ready to start at 3 A.M. this morn. from camp we drew 1/3 d loaf of bread & one small cracker to a man yesterday morning with a promise from the garter master that we should have the rest that night . . .

C. W. Had.

ဆာ

On board the Atlantic Steamboat Ohio River July 1st.

Our journey from Nashville was a quite pleasant one we passed through several places of note viz bowling green. . . . We reached Louisville about 3 Oclock A.M. were marched through the city to Newport two miles down the river & put aboard this boat . . .

C. W. H.

ဆာ

Cario Ill. July 3rd board the Steam boat Atlantic. 9½ A.M.

We arrived here yesterday at dusk. Our Journey so far has been a pleasant one, we have orders to get ready to leave the boat. I am ready.

C. W. H.

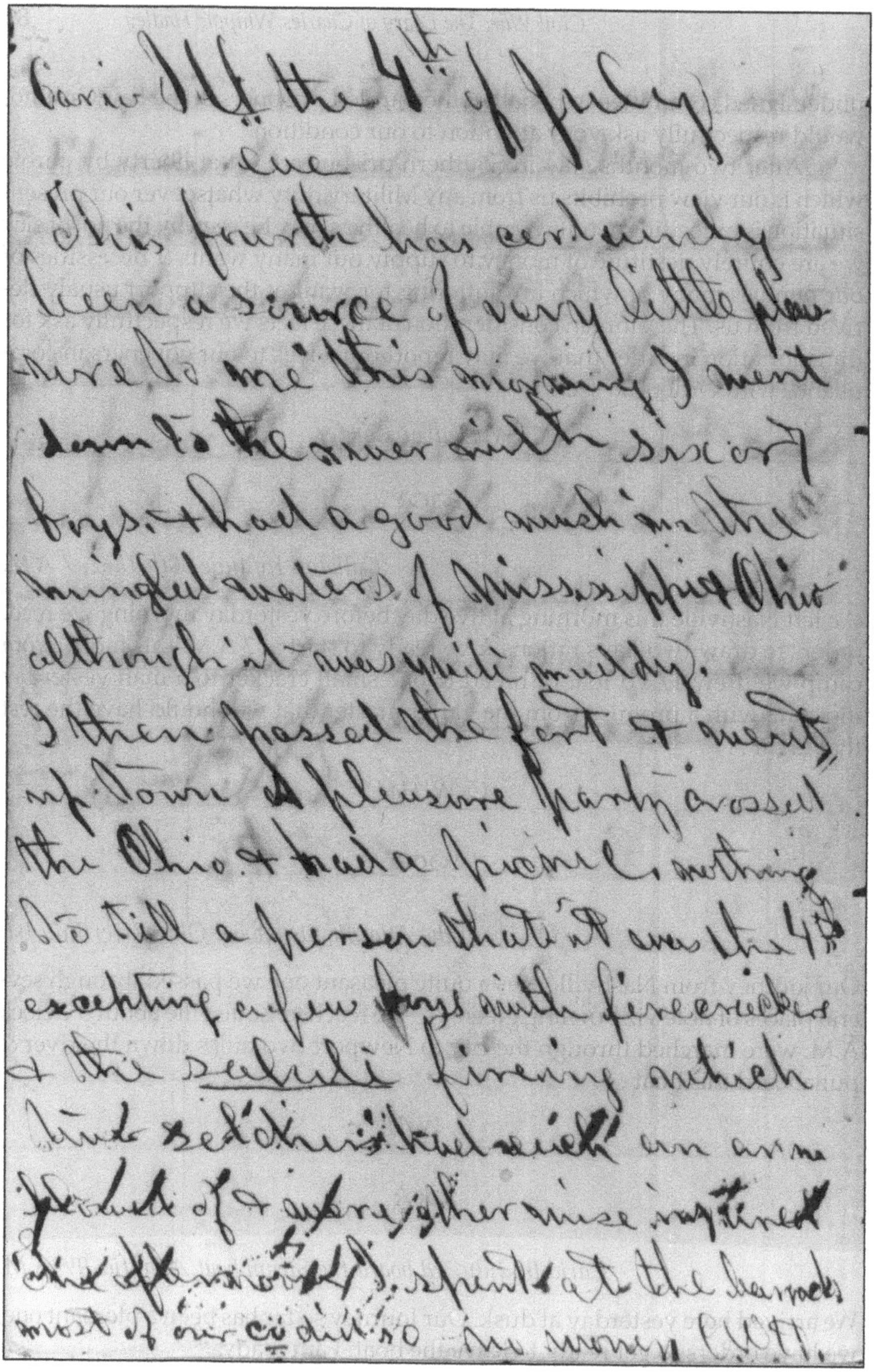

FIGURE 6.4 Hadley's diary entry for July 4, 1862. (L. Tom Perry Special Collections, Harold B. Lee Library, Brigham Young University, MSS 177)

ॐ)ल्ल

July 3d Dusk Barracks west of Cario ½ m

We were marched here this afternoon the barracks are a miserable set of houses, the smell is awful. I hope our stay is short It is said that we are to be mustered out . . .

ॐ)ल्ल

Cario Ill. the 4th of July eve

This fourth has certainly been a source of very little pleasure to me this morning I went down to the river with six or 7 boys, & had a good wash in the mingled waters of Mississippi & Ohio although it was quite muddy . . . nothing to tell a person that it was the 4th excepting a few boys with fire crackers & the salute firing which two soldiers had each an arm blowed of & were otherwise injured . . .

C. W. H.

ॐ)ल्ल

Camp Cario (Cairo) Ill. July 9th 1862.

This morning we recd. orders to be ready to move on board Steamboat to St. Louis, we are all ready, what this move is for we have no idea, we expect to go in a short time.

C. W. Hadley.

ॐ)ल्ल

Benton Barracks St. Louis July 12

Here we are again after the lapse of six months during which time we have seen & experienced soldiers life in all it forms & privations. we have passed through the teribl act, <u>Battle,</u> thrice two months we have spent in the dungons of the enemies of our country part of two months were spent within our lins without any object or end, without doing any duty . . .

In the Classroom

Chronological Thinking

- Create a time line of the significant events in Hadley's diary.
- Describe how public opinion toward the war, both North and South, changed between the years 1861–1865.

Historical Comprehension

- Trace Hadley's movements during the period of his diary on a historical map.
- Write a letter from Hadley's perspective to your hometown newspaper describing your experiences in the Union Army.

Historical Analysis and Interpretation

- List the reasons young men on both sides of the Civil War enlisted and describe how these motives differed.
- Write a fictionalized conversation between Hadley and one of his Southern prison guards.

Historical Research Capabilities

- Potential Topics:
  Ulysses S. Grant   Fort Donelson
  Battle of Shiloh   Prisoner of war camps
  Fort Sumter
  Different names of the war ("War of Northern Aggression,"
  "War Between the States")

Historical Issues-Analysis and Decision-Making

- Analyze the significant causes of the Civil War.
- Theorize as to what the United States would look like today had the Civil War not been fought.

7

Slave Narratives from the Federal Writers' Project

"I seed him git one whippin' and nothin' I can do 'cept stand dere and cry. Dey gits whippin's every time massa feels cross. One slave name Bob Love, when massa start to whip him he cuts his throat and dives into de river. He am dat scairt of a whippin' dat he kilt himself." No textbook can convey the misery and suffering, the degradation and humiliation, the deprivation and despair that was the slave experience. The horrors of slavery are best heard through the voices of those who endured.

"Dey didn't larn us nothin' and iffen you did larn to write, you better keep it to yourself, 'cause some slaves got de thumb or finger cut off for larnin' to write." Historians must rely almost entirely on reminiscent accounts to learn about slavery from those who experienced it, for narratives written by slaves during the time of their enslavement are extremely rare. For the few slaves who could read or write, the punishment for using those skills was, as evidenced by the quotation above, swift and severe. The threat of reprisal, however, did not stop slaves from yearning for an education. "In most of us colored folks was the great desire to be able to read and write. We took advantage of every opportunity to educate ourselves."

The relief and satisfaction felt by the ex-slaves at having the opportunity to describe what their lives were like under the "peculiar institution" are readily apparent in the narratives. The inhumane living and working conditions, the cruel treatment meted out by slave owners, the separation of children and parents, and reactions to freedom take on greater meaning and more poignancy when retold in the words of the ex-slaves themselves.

The conditions under which slaves lived are impossible to conceive of today. "We arose from four to five O'clock in the morning and parents and children were given hard work, lasting until nightfall gaves us our respite." "Weht barefoot summer and winter till the feets crack open." "At mealtime they hand me a piece of cornbread and tell me 'Run 'long.' Sometime I git a little piece of meat and biscuit, 'bout onct a month. I gathered up scraps the white chillens lef."

Slaves lived under the constant threat of whippings and beatings. "He made me hold a light, while he whipped her and then made one of the slaves pour salt water on her bleeding back. My innerds turn yet at that sight." "Iffen they was bad they might git whuppin's, but not too hard, not to de bloom. Iffen dey was still bad, dey puts chains on dem and puts dem in de stocks, 'cause there wasn't no jail there."

Perhaps most heartbreaking are the ex-slaves' descriptions of being separated from their parents. "I can't describe the heartbreak and horror of that separation. I was only six years old and it was the last time I ever saw my mother for longer than one night. Twelve children taken away from my mother in one day." "The tears are on my face a long time after the leaving. I was hoping all the time to see Mammy again, but that's the last time."

Even though the ex-slaves are recalling events that occurred more than seventy years before, memories of emancipation are still fresh and clear. "When mother hear that she say she slip out the chimney corner and crack her heels together four times and shouts, 'I's free, I's free.' Then she runs to the field, 'gainst marster's will and tol' all the other slaves and they quit work." "Was I happy? Law Miss. You can take anything. No matter how good you treat it—it wants to be free. You can treat it good and feed it good and give it everything it seems to want—but if you open the cage—it's happy."

The oral histories of former slaves presented here are only seven of the more than over 2,300 collected in seventeen states during the depression years of 1936–1938 by employees of the Federal Writers' Project, a component of the Works Progress Administration. Originally conceived to use unemployed blue-collar workers on public-works projects, the WPA also hired unemployed white-collar workers. The Federal Writers' Project was designed to assist out-of-work writers to utilize their professional skills. Perhaps best remembered for its American Guide series, the Slave Narrative Collection is its most lasting legacy. The 2,300 voices will remain a constant and lasting reminder of the American slave experience.

Source for Slave Narratives, pp. 87–96: *Born in slavery: Slave narratives from the Federal Writers' Project, 1936–1938* (Library of Congress, Manuscript Division).

℘ *Slave Narratives* ℘

Interview with Mr. John W. Fields, Ex-Slave of the Civil War period. September 17, 1937

"My name is John W. Fields and I'm eighty-nine (89) years old. I was born on March 27, 1848 in Owensburg, Ky. That's 115 miles below Louisville, Ky. There was 11 other children besides myself in my family. When I was six years old, all of us children were taken from my parents, because my master died and his estate had to be settled. We slaves were divided by this method. Three disinterested persons were chosen to come to the plantation and together they wrote the names of the different heirs on a few slips of paper. These slips were put in a hat and passed among us slaves. Each one took a slip and the name on the slip was the new owner. I happened to draw the name of a relative of my master who was a widow. I can't describe the heartbreak and horror of that separation. I was only six years old and it was the last time I ever saw my mother for longer than one night. Twelve children taken away from my mother in one day. Five sisters and two brothers went to Charleston, Virginia, one brother and one sister went to Lexington, Ky., one sister went to Hartford, Ky., and one brother and myself stayed in Owensburg, Ky. My mother was later allowed to visit among us children for one week of each year, so she could only remain a short time at each place.

"My life prior to that time was filled with heart-aches and despair. We arose from four to five O'clock in the morning and parents and children were given hard work, lasting until nightfall gaves us our respite. After a meager supper, we generally talked until we grew sleepy, we had to go to bed. Some of us would read, if we were lucky enough to know how.

"In most of us colored folks was the great desire to able to read and write. We took advantage of every opportunity to educate ourselves. The greater part of the plantation owners were very harsh if we were caught trying to learn or write. It was the law that if a white man was caught trying to educate a negro slave, he was liable to prosecution entailing a fine of fifty dollars and a jail sentence. We were never allowed to go to town and it was not until after I ran away that I knew that they sold anything but slaves, tobacco and wiskey. Our ignorance was the greatest hold the South had on us. We knew we could run away, but what then? An offender guilty of this crime was subjected to very harsh punishment.

"When my masters estate had been settled, I was to go with the widowed relative to her place, she swung me up on her horse behind her and promised me all manner of sweet things if I would come peacefully. I didn't fully realize what was happening, and before I knew it, I was on my way to my new home. Upon arrival her manner changed very much, and she took me down to where there was a bunch of men burning brush. She said, "see these

children taken from my mother in one day. Five sisters and two brothers
went to Charleston, Virginia, one brother and one sister went to Lexington,
Ky., one sister went to Hartford, Ky., and one brother and myself
stayed in Owensburg, Ly. My mother was later allowed to visit among
us children for one week of each year, so she could only remain a short
time at each place.

My life prior to that time was filled with heart-aches and despair. We arose from four to five O'clock in the morning and parents
and children were given hard work, lasting until nightfall gaves us
our respite. After a meager supper, we generally talked until we
grew sleepy, we had to go to bed. Some of us would read, if we were
lucky enough to know how.

In most of us colored folks was the great desire to able to read
and write. We took advantage of every opportunity to educate ourselves.
The greater part of the pla tation owners were very harsh if we were
caught trying to learn or write. It was the law that if a white man
was caught try to educate a negro slave, he was liable to prosecution
entailing a fine of fifty dollars and a jail sentence. We were never allowed
to go to town and it was not until after I ran away that I knew that they
sold anything but slaves, tobacco and wiskey. Our ignorance was the
greatest hold the South had on us. We knew we could run away, but what
then? An offender guilty of this crime was subjected to very harsh
punishment.

When my masters estate had been settled, I was to go with the widowed
relative to her place, she swung me up on her horse behind her and promised me all manner of sweet things if I would come peacefully. I didn't
fully realise what was happening, and before I knew it, I was on my
way to my new home. Upon arrival her manner changed very much, and she took

---

FIGURE 7.1   Typescript of John W. Field's oral history. (Library of Congress
Manuscript Division)

men?" I said, yes. Well, go help them, she replied. So at the age of six I started my life as an independent slave. From then on my life as a slave was a repetition of hard work, poor quarters and board. We had no beds at that time, we just "bunked" on the floor. I had one blanket and manys the night I sat by the fireplace during the long cold nights in the winter.

"My mistress had separated me from all my family but one brother with sweet words, but that pose was dropped after she reached her place. Shortly after I had been there, she married a northern man by the name of David Hill. At first he was very nice to us, but he gradually acquired a mean and overbearing manner toward us. I remember one incident that I don't like to remember. One of the women slaves had been very sick and she was unable to work just as fast as he thought she ought to. He had driven her all day with no results. That night after completeing our work he called us all together. He made me hold a light, while he whipped her and then made one of the slaves pour salt water on her bleeding back. My innerds turn yet at that sight.

"At the beginning of the Civil War I was still at this place as a slave. It looked at the first of the war as if the south would win, as most of the big battles were won by the South. This was because we slaves stayed at home and tended the farms and kept their families.

"To eliminate this solid support of the South, the Emancipation Act was passed, freeing all the slaves. Most of the slaves were so ignorant they did not realize they were free. The planters knew this and as Kentucky never seceeded from the Union, they would send slaves into Kentucky from other states in the south and hire them out to plantations. For these reasons I did not realize that I was free untill 1864. I immediately resolved to run away and join the Union Army and so my brother and I went to Owensburg, Ky. and tried to join. My brother was taken, but I was refused as being too young. I tried at Evansville, Terre Haute and Indianaoplis but was unable to get in. I then tried to find work and was finally hired by a man at $7.00 a month. That was my first independent job. From then on I went from one job to another working as general laborer.

℘℘

EX-SLAVE STORIES
(Texas)

> TEMPIE CUMMINS was born at Brookeland, Texas, sometime before the Civil War, but does not know her exact age. William Neyland owned Tempie and her parents. She now lives alone in a small, weatherbeaten shack in the South Quarters, a section of Jasper, Tex.

"They call me Tempie Cummins and I was born at Brookeland but I don' know jus' the 'xact date. My father's name was Jim Starkins and my mother's name was Charlotte Brooks and both of 'em came from Alabama. I had jus' one brudder, Bill, and four sisters named Margaret and Hannah and Mary and 'Liza. Life was good when I was with them and us play round. Miss Fannie Neyland, she Mis' Phil Scarborough now, she raises me, 'cause I was give to them when I was eight year old.

"I slep' on a pallet on the floor. They give me a homespun dress onct a year at Christmas time. When company come I had to run and slip on that dress. At other time I wore white chillens' cast-off clothes so wore they was ready to throw away. I had to pin them up with red horse thorns to hide my nakedness. My dress was usually split from hem to neck and I had to wear them till they was strings. Weht barefoot summer and winter till the feets crack open.

"I never seed my grandparents 'cause my mother she sold in Alabama when she's 17 and they brung her to Texas and treat her rough. At mealtime they hand me a piece of cornbread and tell me 'Run 'long.' Sometime I git a little piece of meat and biscuit, 'bout onct a month. I gathered up scraps the white chillens lef'.

FIGURE 7.2 Store used for auctioning slaves, Atlanta, Georgia, 1861. (Library of Congress, Prints & Photographs Division, Selected Civil War photographs, LC-B8171-3608)

"Marster was rough. He take two beech switches and twist them together and whip 'em to a stub. Many's the time I's bled from them whippin's. Our old mistus, she try to be good to us, I reckon, but she was turrible lazy. She had two of us to wait on her and then she didn' treat us good.

"Marster had 30 or 40 acres and he raise cotton, and corn and 'tatoes. He used to raise 12 bales cotton a year and then drink it all up. We work from daylight till dark, and after. Marster punish them what didn' work hard enough.

"The white chillen tries to teach me to read and write but I didn' larn much, cause I allus workin'. Mother was workin' in the house, and she cooked too. She say she used to hide in the chimney corner and listen to what the white folks say. When freedom was 'clared, marster wouldn' tell 'em, but mother she hear him tellin' mistus that the slaves was free but they didn' know it and he's not gwineter tell 'em till he makes another crop or two. When mother hear that she say she slip out the chimney corner and crack her heels together four times and shouts, 'I's free, I's free.' Then she runs to the field, 'gainst marster's will and tol' all the other slaves and they quit work. Then she run away and in the night she slip into a big ravine near the house and have them bring me to her. Marster, he come out with his gun and shot at mother but she run down the ravine and gits away with me.

℘ℛ

EX-SLAVE STORIES
(Texas)

> SARAH BENJAMIN, 82, was born
> a slave of the Gilbert family,
> in Clavin Parish, Louisiana.
> In 1867 she married Cal Benj-
> amin and they settled in Cors-
> icana, Texas, where Sarah now
> lives.

"I is Sarah Benjamin and is 82 year old, 'cause my mammy told me I's born in 1855 in Clavin Parish in Louisiana. Her name was Fannie and my pappy's name was Jack Callahan. There was jus' three of us chillen and I's de oldest.

"Marse Gilbert was tol'able good to we'uns, and give us plenty to eat. He had a smokehouse as big as a church and it was full, and in de big kitchen we all et, chillen and all. De grown folks et first and den de chillen. Did we have plenty of possums and fish by de barrels full! All dis was cooked in de racks over de fireplace and it were good.

"Our clothes was all homespun and de shoes were made by de shoemaker. Old marse wanted all of us to go to church and if dey didn't have shoes dey have something like de moccasin.

"I don't know how many slaves there was, but it was a lot, maybe 60 or 70. Dey worked hard every day 'cept Sunday. Iffen they was bad they might git whuppin's, but not too hard, not to de bloom. Iffen dey was still bad, dey puts chains on dem and puts dem in de stocks, 'cause there wasn't no jail there.

"Once when I's little, marse stripped me stark modern naked and puts me on de block, but he wouldn't sell me, 'cause he was bid only $350.00 and he says no, 'cause I was good and fat.

"Dey didn't larn us nothin' and iffen you did larn to write, you better keep it to yourself, 'cause some slaves got de thumb or finger cut off for larnin' to write. When de slaves come in from de fields dey didn't larn mothin', they jus' go to bed, 'lessen de moonshine nights come and dey could work in de tobacco patch. De marster give each one de little tobacco patch and iffen he raised more'n he could use he could sell it.

℘℘℘

Oklahoma Writers' project
Revision of story sent in 8-13-37
JOHN WHITE
Age 121 years
Sand Springs, Okla.

Of all my Mammy's children I am the first born and the longest living. The others all gone to join Mammy. She was named Mary White, the same name as her Mistress, the wife of my first master, James White.

About my pappy. I never hear his name and I never see him, not even when I was the least child around the old Master's place 'way back there in Georgia more'n one-hundred twenty years ago!

Mammy try to make it clear to me about my daddy. She married like the most of the slaves in them days.

He was a slave on another plantation. One day he come for to borrow something from Master White. He sees a likely looking gal, and the way it work out that gal was to be my Mammy. After that he got a paper saying it was all right for him to be off his own plantation. He come a'courting over to Master Whites. After a while he talks with the Master. Says he wants to marry the gal, Mary. The Master says it's all right if it's all right with Mary and the other white folks. He finds out it is and they makes ready for the wedding.

Mary says a preacher wedding is the best but Master say he can marry them just as good. There wasn't no Bible, just an old Almanac. Master White read something out of that. That's all and they was married. The wedding was over!

Every night he gets a leave paper from his Master and come over to be with his wife, Mary. The next morning he leaves her to work in the fields. Then one night Mammy says he don't come home. The next night is the same, and the next. From then on Mammy don't see him no more—never find out what happen to my pappy.

When I was born Mammy named me John, John White. She tells me I was the blackest 'white' boy she ever see! I stays with her till I was eleven year old. The Master wrote down in the book when I was born, April 10, 1816, and I know it's right. Mammy told me so, and Master told me when I was eleven and he sold me to Sarah Davenport.

Mistress Sarah lived in Texas. Master White always selling and trading to folks all over the country. I hates to leave on account of Mammy and the good way Master White fared the slaves—they was good people. Mammy cry but I has to go just the same. The tears are on my face a long time after the leaving. I was hoping all the time to see Mammy again, but that's the last time.

℘)℘

EX-SLAVE STORIES
(Texas)

> WALTER RIMM, 80, was born a slave
> of Captain Hatch, in San Patricio
> County, Texas. After Walter was
> freed, he helped his father farm
> for several years, then worked
> as a cook for fifteen years on
> the King Ranch. He moved to Fort
> Worth and cooked for Mrs. Arthur
> Goetz for twenty-five years. He
> lives at 913 E. Second St., Fort
> Worth.

"You wants to know 'bout slavery? Well, I's had a deal happen 'sides dat, but I's born on Captain Hatch's plantation, 'cross de bay from Corpus Christi. He had somewheres near fifty slaves, and mammy told me he buyed her in Tennessee and pappy in South Carolina. Massa Hatch buys and sells niggers some dem days, but he ain't a nigger trader.

"Dem sales am onething what make de 'pression on me. I hears de old folks whisper 'bout gwine have de sale and 'bout noon dere am a crowd of white folks in de front yard and a nigger trader with he slaves. Dey sets up a platform in middle de yard and one white man gits on dat and 'nother white man comes up and has a white woman with him. She 'pears to be 'bout fifteen years old and has long, black hair down her back. Dey puts her on de platform and den I hears a scream, and a woman what look like de gal, cries out, 'I'll cut my throat if my daughter am sold.' De white man goes and talks to her, and fin'ly 'lows her to take de young gal away with her. Dat sho' stirs up some

FIGURE 7.3 Walter Rimm, age 80. (Library of Congress, Prints & Photographs Division, Forms part of Portraits of African American ex-slaves from the U.S. Works Progress Administration, Federal Writers' Project slave narratives collections LC-USZ62-125336)

'motion 'mongst de white folks, but dey say dat gal have jus' a li'l nigger blood and can be sold for a slave, but she look white as anybody I ever seed . . .

"Massa and missus took dey goodness by spells like. Sometimes dey was hard to git 'long with and sometimes dey was easy to git 'long with. I don't know de cause, but it am so. De mostest trouble am 'bout de work. Dey wants you to work if you can or can't. My pappy have de back mis'ry and many de time I seed him crawl to de grist mill. Him am buyed 'cause him am de good millhand. He tells us his pappy am white, and dat one reason he am de run-awayer. I's scairt all de time, 'cause he run away. I seed him git one whippin' and nothin' I can do 'cept stand dere and cry. Dey gits whippin's every time massa feels cross. One slave name Bob Love, when massa start to whip him he cuts his throat and dives into de river. He am dat scairt of a whippin' dat he kilt himself.

"My pappy wasn't 'fraid of nothin'. He am light cullud from de white blood, and he runs away sev'ral times. Dere am big woods all round and we sees lots of run-awayers. One old fellow name John been a run-awayer for four years and de patterrollers tries all dey tricks, but dey can't cotch him. Dey wants him bad, 'cause it 'spire other slaves to run away if he stays a-loose. Dey sots de trap for him. Dey knows he like good eats, so dey 'ranges for a quiltin' and gives chitlin's and lye hominy. John comes and am inside when de patterrollers rides up to de door. Everybody gits quiet and John stands near de door, and when dey starts to come in he grabs de shovel full of hot ashes and throws dem into de patterrollers faces. He gits through and runs off, hollerin', 'Bird in de air!'

"One woman named Rhodie runs off for long spell. De hounds won't hunt her. She steals hot light bread when dey puts it in de window to cool, and lives on dat. She told my mammy how to keep de hounds from followin' you is to take black pepper and put it in you socks and run without you shoes. It make de hounds sneeze.

℘ℭ

Ida Blackshear Hutchinson
Death of Sixty Babies

"They was too many babies to leave in the quarters for some one to take care of during the day. When the young mothers went to work, Blackshear had them take their babies with them to the field, and it was two or three miles from the house to the field. He didn't want them to lose time walking backward and forward nursing. They built a long old trough like a great long old cradle and put all these babies in it every morning when the mother come out to the field. It was set at the end of the rows under a big old cottonwood tree.

"When they were at the other end of the row, all at once a cloud no bigger than a small spot came up, and it grew fast, and it thundered and lightened as if the world were coming to an end, and the rain just came down in great sheets. And when it got so they could go to the other end of the field, that trough was filled with water and every baby in it was floating 'round in the water drownded. They never got nary a lick of labor and nary a red penny for any one of them babies.

℘ℭ

Tom Robinson

"One day I was out milking the cows. Mr. Dave come down into the field, and he had a paper in his hand. 'Listen to me, Tom,' he said, 'listen to what I reads you.' And he read from a paper all about how I was free. You can't tell how I felt. 'You're jokin' me.' I says. 'No, I ain't,' says he. 'You're free.' 'No,' says I, 'it's a joke.' 'No,' says he, 'it's a law that I got to read this paper to you. Now listen while I read it again.'

"But still I wouldn't believe him. 'Just go up to the house,' says he, 'and ask Mrs. Robinson. She'll tell you.' So I went. 'It's a joke,' I says to her. 'Did you ever know your master to tell you a lie?' she says. 'No,' says I, 'I ain't.' 'Well,' she says, 'the war's over and you're free.'

"By that time I thought maybe she was telling me what was right. 'Miss Robinson,' says I, 'can I go over to see the Smiths?'—they was a colored family that lived nearby. 'Don't you understand,' says she, 'you're free. You don't have to ask me what you can do. Run along child.'

"And so I went. And do you know why I was a 'going? I wanted to find out if they was free too. I just couldn't take it all in. I couldn't believe we was all free alike.

"Was I happy? Law Miss. You can take anything. No matter how good you treat it—it wants to be free. You can treat it good and feed it good and give it everything it seems to want—but if you open the cage—it's happy.

In the Classroom

Chronological Thinking
- Create a time line of significant events in the history of slavery in the United States.
- Describe how the feelings and attitudes of slaves changed after emancipation.

Historical Comprehension
- Explain why the institution of slavery prospered in the South.
- Write a narrative describing the daily life of a slave.

Historical Analysis and Interpretation
- Write a newspaper article from the perspective of a southerner in 1860 describing why slavery is important to Southerners and the economics of the South.
- Write five to ten questions you would ask the ex-slaves given the opportunity.

Historical Research Capabilities
- Potential Topics:

Slavery	the Underground Railroad
Emancipation Proclamation	Federal Writers' Project
New Deal	Works Progress Administration

Historical Issues-Analysis and Decision-Making
- Analyze the content of the narratives given the fact that almost all the writers who interviewed the ex-slaves were white.
- Describe what options slaves had to their enslavement and the consequences to alternative courses of actions.

8

Immigration: The Diary of Swen Magnus Swensson

"After many difficulties at the emigration office, I am finally down at the steamship *Calypso*, which waits majestically to transport its costly cargo of several hundred people to a distant land." Swen Swensson, a twenty-three year old engineering student, was just moments away from leaving his Swedish homeland. "The ship's bells sound and the gang plank is released. Slowly and ceremoniously the large boat leaves Sweden's second largest city while handkerchiefs wave and cries of cheer are heard from both land the boat."

From all over Europe, millions of people left their native countries in the early part of the twentieth century, immigrating to the United States to escape the ravages of famine and disease, to avoid political or religious persecution, or because of agricultural setbacks. Regardless of their age, gender, religion, ethnicity, or country of origin, their unifying belief was simple: life would be better in the "promised land" of the United States.

Swen Swensson's journey began on October 18, 1907 and was caused by family financial difficulties that made it impossible for him to complete his engineering degree. Swensson's final destination was Salt Lake City, Utah, home to his sister who had sent him money for third-class passage. He arrived on November 7. "I got to the home of my dear ones here about 9 o'clock and surprised them before they were ready for bed." The diary left by the well-educated, literate Swensson describes one immigrant's experience.

From Göteborg, Swensson traveled by steamship to Hull, England and then by train to Southampton where he boarded the *RMS Adriatic* for the transatlantic crossing. The ship clearly impressed the young engineering student "The size of the boat is overwhelming. . . . Its smokestacks are so big that if one of them were lying on the ground, two locomotives could meet side by side in it. That is, it is as large as a double-track tunnel. . . . The *Adriatic* is 726 feet long."

Among the two thousand passengers on board were immigrants from nearly every country in Europe. "There is quite a conglomeration of people on board now: Swedes, Norwegians, Danes, Finns, Germans, Englishmen, Irish, Frenchmen, Italians, Turks, Americans, Swiss, Austrians, and others, and it all makes for a genuine tower of babel." Most immigrants could only afford third-class travel, meaning few amenities were present. "In the travel handbook it had been advertised that we in third-class would have a conversation lounge, smoking lounge, bathroom, and access to a barber; but I did not see any."

Swensson was obviously an outgoing young man who found and enjoyed a variety of activities to pass the time during the voyage. "I played some patriotic songs and induced my countrymen and women to demonstrate that they were gifted with nice voices and in addition, they sang in the world's most beautiful language— Swedish." A transatlantic crossing without bad weather was very rare. "The masts are whining and the ship is rocking. . . . There is a terrible storm today . . . the waves are like small mountains."

Imagine the joy, relief, and fear experienced by immigrants as New York City came into view. "Several lighthouses blink their welcome to the port after a long and tiring trip. The reflections from New York's millions of lights greet us first. Now everyone is hanging over the railing and nobody bothers to do anything else." "We can hardly see the buildings or houses, only the thousands of lit windows from the great skyscrapers and the impressive signs with words and names in gas flames."

"We were, you see, brought out on a ferry, trunks and all, to a place that is called Ellis Island to undergo a lot of things." During its years of operation from 1892 to 1954, over twelve million immigrants first stepped foot on U.S. soil at Ellis Island. The long, confusing process of entering the United States began with a medical examination. "First we came to a doctor to be inspected once more; and if we passed, we could continue." Pronounced healthy by the doctor, Swensson continued to the legal inspection, where his financial fitness to enter the country was assessed. "He asked me where I was going, if I had any relatives or friends who would receive me, what I was going to do in this country, and how much money I had with me. Since I answered all of the questions satisfactorily, I was allowed to continue."

Swensson was still only halfway to his final destination when he arrived in New York and the long train trip west afforded Swensson his first opportunity to observe both the country and its inhabitants.

The U.S. landscape impressed him. "The train rushes through very beautiful countryside with low, wooded hills." "Up on the mountains the view is marvelous. There are even more mountain ranges, the snow-covered peaks of which glitter in the sun." Swenson's impression of Americans was decidedly more mixed. "Toward afternoon a lot of American youngsters came into our compartment . . . I was invited by them to have coffee and sandwiches." "I entered a car where there was a lot of room; but they drove me out, saying that they were clean Americans and did not want any foreigners near them."

Swensson's assimilation into American society and culture was successful. He met his wife, Hilma Nelson, in Salt Lake City and together they raised three children. After a long career as an engineer in the steel industry, Swensson and his wife retired to Waupaca, Wisconsin, where the countryside reminded them both of their native Sweden.

ᔓ *The Diary of Swen Magnus Swensson* ᔕ

October 18:   After many difficulties at the emigration office, I am finally down at the steamship *Calypso*, which waits majestically to transport its costly cargo of several hundred people to a distant land. The rain is pouring and we have to get shelter in the baggage area in order not to get soaked during the long wait to get on board. First- and second-class passengers, who customarily have things good, are the first to board—not that I am impatient to leave my dear homeland—especially not since I have the happiness of being followed by my dear brother and one of my cousins; but because it is going to happen and it is also raining, it is best to be on my way, the sooner the better. Finally, the ship's bells sound and the gang plank is released. Slowly and ceremoniously the large boat leaves Sweden's second largest city while handkerchiefs wave and cries of cheer are heard from both land the boat. Soon the figures of our dear friends and the church steeples of Göteborg disappear in the distance . . .

I spent the afternoon making acquaintances. On the foredeck a lively dance to accordion music is taking place. A steward comes and announces that food is being served; and since one gets very hungry in nice weather out at sea, we hurry down to the dining room expecting to get something really good. But if it was crowded on the stairs, it is even more so down below. After countless shoves, I finally elbowed my way forward to the table and

Swensson, Swen Magnus; Jarvi, Raymond, ed.; Strombeck, Rita, transl. An emigrant's journey to America in 1907. *Swedish-American Historical Quarterly*, 1989, 40(4): 184–207. © Swedish-American Historical Society.

was served coffee with sugar and cream. Then we got a few slices of bread with something special that they called butter—but it was not really Swedish butter, I noticed. I tasted the coffee and was relieved that I did not have to drink all of it. I ate a little of the bread and the so-called butter; but since they probably would not have anything to make pudding out of the next day—and I saw others thinking the same thing—I left half of it, which was carefully taken back . . .

℘℞

October 19:   . . . I went up on deck to get some fresh air; but this was easier said than done since I had to pass the foredeck in order to get to the upper deck. On the foredeck the waves were splashing very high, but not so high that I could not get by—yet enough so that I got soaked. I ran between two waves and finally got up where it was nice. The air down below was repulsive. But even on the upper deck the waves were splashing. I got very wet from one of them. There are not many passengers on deck today. Most prefer to remain below. Even I began to feel an unpleasant sensation in my stomach, but then I took out some apples and pears that my thoughtful brother had given me and soon I felt better. If they had made pudding from the remainder of the bread slices, I would not eat it because I did not feel up to it. I took a few potatoes and a piece of herring. Instead of a knife and a fork, I used my fingers; but even these things did not taste good. Yet this was supposed to be effective in preventing seasickness.

Towards evening there were many on deck, so we had a dance. The musician, a happy fellow from Göteborg, disappeared every half hour but then came back and continued to play. I assume that one can guess the reason. The girls would leave to get a drink, they said, but they had a difficult time keeping their drinks down. Evening came even on this stormy day, and it was a lovely evening in its own way. Seeing the ocean in turmoil when a full moon is shining in a cloudless sky and the stars are out, too, is a sight that I promise I shall not soon forget. I sat for hours marveling at this vision, and here and there small groups of people were singing "Du gamla du fria" or "Várt land," among other songs. Soon we heard the inevitable, "Everyone in bed;" and we had to—although with heavy hearts—go down to the stuffy lower decks . . .

℘℞

October 20:   . . . I got dressed quickly because there were interesting things to expect. We were supposed to get to England in the morning, it was said. About 9 o'clock we saw once more a blue strip in the distance and a lot of coastal boats sailing in all possible directions. These are the shores of Scotland. Another few hours and we shall come to the port of Hull. The sea is filled with boats of all nationalities—we even see some Swedish ones.

Now we are nearing the dock and the city is becoming more visible. With black and burnt-down houses all over, it gives a very dismal impression. Finally we glide into the dock. About thirty curious Englishmen are standing on the quay. But why is it so unusually ceremonious and quite? No seagulls are heard, no noisy cranes in spite of the fact that about 100 vessels are waiting to unload their cargo. Now I remember that it is Sunday and there are perhaps no people in the world who honor the Sabbath more than the English. They believe in the reformed teachings, which are very strict . . .

ℰℐℭℛ

October 21:   Well, it is now 4 o'clock in the morning. It is probably best that I get up. I cannot avoid the trouble of getting dressed, but I had also better wash and comb my hair so that the Englishmen will not get too bad an impression of Swedes. Then we were supposed to get "coffee," but what that meant was a rather disguised hot water.

Imagine how nice, we get to ride to the railway station in large busses. They come to fetch us and our baggage, and then they take off so fast that I thought they would overturn. I sat on the top deck. Busses and streetcars here have seats both inside and on their tops. Since some of us were going to Liverpool and others to Southampton, we would be taking different trains. It took several hours until we were ready for our trip. We had to have tickets and in order to get them, we had to have our travel papers. I even had time to go to a barbershop. Most of them would not open until 1 o'clock p.m., but I did find one that opened at 9. It took much longer to get a shave here than it does in Sweden. They had so many perfumes and ointments, and one even had to lie down to be shaved. It cost about 30 *öre* in our money.

Finally the train departed, but before that we said farewell to those who were traveling to Liverpool. They were taking the White Star Line, which leaves from that city, and the others would go with the Cunard and Atlantic lines. We traveled to London, which was our first stop. The train went unbelievably fast, but there were special ties and supports on both sides so this was possible. In spite of the fact that our train went so fast, another came on the second track (it was a double track) and caught up with us, passed by, and disappeared ahead of us. The English countryside was rather beautiful in its way; we traveled mostly through plains. There were many fertile fields that seemed to be well taken care of; they were all enclosed with hedges of hawthorne, nicely pruned. It seemed very pleasant. Even on both sides of the tracks, hawthorne hedges had been planted. All of the houses, even out in the countryside, were of brick. The barns were rather small and serve only to have animals in, while all the hay and straw was gathered in piles. Even the barns were of brick. The houses have a very strange style, almost always two levels, usually with chimneys on the roofs, spread here and there without any particular order. The smoke pipes are always raised high above the chimneys. I have lately seen in Sweden that they have adopted this ugly style, for example, the minister's house in Trollhättan.

People are starting to get sleepy on the train, and we are eager to be in Southampton. Finally at 7 o'clock we arrive here, when everything is dark. No busses come to meet us, but rather we must find our own way to the emigrant hotel. A lovely table with clean, white napkins and a tablecloth had been prepared, and polite waiters served us an excellent meal—the best since we had left Göteborg. After we had eaten to the point of satisfaction, some of us went out to see the city, while others gathered in a room, played the piano, and sang spiritual and patriotic songs. I did the first thing and then the other. Southampton is a city of about 300,000 inhabitants, but I did not think that it was as large as Stockholm, which has an equal number. The houses were usually very ugly here, but once in a while there was a nice one. The hotel and some of the steamship line buildings were pretty. The business streets were broad and clean. On both sides there were large shops with display windows that took up whole walls, and they usually presented what they had to sell very nicely. There were many fruit stores. These had almost half of their goods out on the sidewalks. I thought it would be easy for someone who wanted to steal to take an apple or a handful of grapes, but this apparently did not happen often, according to what I was told. Finally evening came this day, too, when we had seen so much. I forgot to say that we were reimbursed here for what we had lost of our friends who had gone to Liverpool. We came together with all the people from Denmark, Norway, England, etc. who would be going on the same boat. This was the first evening that I was able to get undressed since I had left Göteborg. Here there were comfortable beds with clean, white linens; and I slept very well the whole night. A technologist and I shared a room with two beds.

෨෬

October 22:   Now I have slept well and since breakfast is served at 7 o'clock it is best to get up. I was a little late for breakfast but was served anyway. The food was still good. today we are going to get boat tickets and the numbers of our cabins. At 5 o'clock we have a physical examination to see if anyone must be sent home. While we are waiting, some of us go down to look at our home for the next few weeks and also to see if our trunks are on board. The size of the boat is overwhelming, and we are really amazed since we are only used to canal boats or other smaller ones. I thought that the *Calypso* was big, but the *Adriatic* is ten times larger. The *Calypso* was 2,300 tons; this one is 25, 000 tons and it is the largest ship this line has. Its smokestacks are so big that if one of them were lying on the ground, two locomotives could meet side by side in it. That is, it is as large as a double-track tunnel. In order to move the rudder, they have a large steam engine with two cylinders, together with another engine in reserve that is just as large. The *Adriatic* is 726 feet long. I shall have to describe it in more detail when I get on board . . .

🕉

October 23:   Today is the big day; we finally get to board the floating hotel called the *Adriatic*. But first we are going to have breakfast, and then wagons will come to fetch our hand luggage. We must walk the long way to the boat. When we got there, we gathered in a huge luggage building, and there we had to wait a very long time before the boat was ready to receive us. Here there were a lot of Italians and other southern Europeans who had not been examined by any doctors, and that had to be done before they could go on board. First- and second-class passengers were boarded, then the baggage, then our hand luggage. Finally we, too, had the honor of going on board. We looked for our cabins with the help of the numbers we had and made ourselves at home . . .

We have been down in the dining room and eaten lunch now, which was pretty good. There were several who complained that they had eaten too much; I was one of them. Different menus are printed every day on the ship's press, and now I shall describe one of them:

> 7 o'clock breakfast: Oatmeal and milk, smoked herring, beefsteak, browned potatoes, freshly baked bread and butter, jam, Swedish bread, tea or coffee.
>
> 1 o'clock dinner: Soup with rice, fresh bread, a kind of large biscuit, jam, roast beef, brown sauce, fresh beans, boiled or browned potatoes, and two oranges every other day.
>
> 5 o'clock tea: Hash, cheese, pickles, fresh bread and butter, rhubarb jam, cooked beans, tea.
>
> 8 o'clock supper: Oatmeal, toast, and cheese.

As you are reading this, you may be thinking, "That is probably very good food;" but the truth is that it sounds better than it tasted. There was always sufficient food; and if one wanted double portions, one also received them. Many were not used to such everyday fare—but there really was no taste to the food, I thought, and others agreed. They had three dining rooms: one for men, one for women, and one for families.

In the evening we would all gather together in one of the dining rooms where there was a piano, and it was used a great deal. There was also an Englishman who played the bassoon, and another Englishman sang many happy songs in his language. I played some patriotic songs and induced my countrymen and women to demonstrate that they were gifted with nice voices and in addition, they sang in the world's most beautiful language—Swedish.

The weather was beautiful, and many preferred to stay on deck as long as they could. We third-class passengers were located on the fore- and after-decks, Second-class passengers occupied half of the middle deck, and the rest of the ship was reserved for the first-class ones. In the travel handbook it had been advertised that we in third-class would have a conversation lounge, smoking lounge, bathroom, and access to a barber; but I did not see any of these amenities . . .

℘Ↄ℞

October 24:   . . . At 1 o'clock we saw land again. This was Ireland. We passed the city of Queenstown. It, too, is situated on a bay, beautifully surrounded by green hills. Rowboats swarmed around our ship, and large paddle steamers loaded with people and baggage came sailing out. It is surprising that this ship can hold so many people; but when all were on board, there was still room for more. When we came to a stop, all the rowboats came to the sides of our ship; and people called up to us to throw down the lines that were on our decks. This we did; and when they got hold of the ends of these lines, they secured old women and baskets and signaled us to pull them up. The women were dangling between water and sky, but finally they were safely on deck. They had their baskets with them, as well and began to sell apples, table-cloths, lace, and so forth. The officers on our ship tried to drive them away, but they simply ran off to another spot and would resume selling there. Finally, when our ship was ready to leave, they scurried to get off it, going back down their lines.

The sun is now shining in a cloudless sky and it is warm; so I am sitting on the deck without an overcoat and am almost sweating. Our ship glides slowly along the coast of Ireland, which is so beautiful. Fields slanting down toward the shores are seen. They look like a chessboard, the lines between the squares that separate the various fields consisting of hawthorne hedges. But soon all of this disappears, and now we head seriously for the land to the west, New York being our next port. There is quite a conglomeration of people on board now: Swedes, Norwegians, Danes, Finns, Germans, Englishmen, Irish, Frenchmen, Italians, Turks, Americans, Swiss, Austrians, and others, and it all makes for a genuine tower of babel. We associate freely with each other and easily make acquaintances; we write down addresses so that we can keep in touch by letter. Everyone is nice, foreigners as well as countrymen. We spends the time reading, promenading arm in arm, and exchanging addresses with the promise of keeping in touch. Those who can dance do so continuously. There probably are not many religious people on board, because there is never any reading of the Bible or spiritual singing. A middle aged woman made several attempts in these directions but got nowhere, because there was no interest. This day, too, ended with music and songs in the lounge.

෨෬

October 26:   The masts are whining and the ship is rocking. Time after time, our little window is darkened by a wave. But we have to get up. . . . There is a terrible storm today. The Swedish Americans who are sailing with us say that they have never experienced such a storm; the waves are like small mountains. Our ship, which is very large, should be able to withstand; but it is lifted up with each wave, almost on end. When it lowers itself so that the front goes down and the stern goes up, the propellers are working in the air and then the whole boat shakes. But then all of a sudden, the stern goes way down and we are surrounded by mountains of water. It can get worse, however, and then passengers will be forbidden to go on deck. Nothing new today.

෨෬

October 27:   Today is Sunday. Even in bed, I can feel that the storm is continuing. My cabin is in the middle of the ship, but I still feel how the boat is shaking. From the life on board, there is little to indicate that this is Sunday. There is no preaching in third-class passage. In second-class there was a sermon that I was able to understand, but we were told to leave.

On the ship there are small groups that have been formed. Some boys have their special girlfriends with whom they stay together. In the evenings, one can see them on a sofa in the corner with a blanket over them. I prefer to associate with foreigners in order to study them. I became good friends with a Norwegian boy and a Danish boy and girl. It was interesting to hear their political opinions. The Irishmen were not particularly attractive, but the Irish girls were very pretty and very nice. The Swiss were a happy group. They sang their alpine songs and laughed unendingly, and their girls loved to play little tricks. The Englishmen were very proud, but they certainly were able to consume food . . .

We now understand that we have traveled half the distance to New York. On maps set up in the dining rooms, the captain marks how far we have gone each day. Now I shall go down and listen to the music, eat some oatmeal, toast, and biscuits, and then go to bed.

෨෬

October 28:   How cold it is today! The previous days have been very warm— even during the storm—but today there is a noticeable difference. This is due to several factors. For the most part, the wind has been from the south or southwest; but today it is from the northwest. Another reason is that we are just off Newfoundland, and that place is supposed to have a cold climate. We have passed the Gulf Stream, having stayed quite close to it; and it carries warm water from warm climates. For those of us who come from the North, the cold is not so bad; but the southerners really suffer . . .

80CR

October 29:   We are still heading westward unceasingly. Imagine how far we now are from our indescribably dear homeland. We have been traveling continuously for fourteen days, always to the west. The same sky, the same faces, the same boat. The ship is large, but our world is small. Every day, telegrams come on the wireless from all parts of the world and from other vessels. I do not recall if I mentioned that the clocks are set back a half hour every day; so when it is 12 o'clock p.m., it becomes 11:30 a.m. Tonight there is a thick fog, so the fog horn is sounded every minute . . .

80CR

October 30:   Now we are getting close enough to see land again. Tomorrow is the big day. Today all those who have not been vaccinated must be. On my church certificate, however, it said that I was all right. There was a long line of people standing with lifted arms to demonstrate that they had the proper marks. Usually the Southerners had not yet been vaccinated.

The crew aboard does good business—even though it is dishonest—by selling food, fruit, and other things that actually belong to the ship. They also take bribes from those who have money and who want more and better food than we others get. This happens even though there are signs all over that it is forbidden.

80CR

October 31:   The weather is beautiful today; the sun is shining clearly in the sky. No one is seasick. Today I have seen many people whom I have not seen previously. They must have been sick during the trip, and only today do they have the energy to get up. It is hoped that today we shall see our longed-for New York. As soon as we come up on deck, all eyes turn toward the west; but still we do not see anything. . . . After lunch was finished, we went back up on deck. We spotted a blue ridge in the distance. It was the coast of the state in America that is called Massachusetts. So we finally got to see the shores of America for the first time. It brought to mind a whole series of mixed feelings.

The blue stripe becomes clearer, and we begin to see land even on the opposite side of the ship. Then I understand that we have reached a bay. It begins to get dark, and after some time in the distance the sky is lit up as if there were a gigantic fire. Several lighthouses blink their welcome to the port after a long and tiring trip. The reflections from New York's millions of lights greet us first. Now everyone is hanging over the railing and nobody bothers to do anything else, excepting for eating dinner, which we cannot afford to miss. Soon we approach a fortress that is called Sandy Hook. Now there comes sailing toward us mail boats to collect our cargo of mail, which reaches land first. Now appears something beautiful, a sight that I cannot describe. What an effect all those lights have. Along the shoreline stretch thousands of long rows of lamps; and in the city, as if it were terraced, one sees lights in all directions, one on top of the other. We can hardly see the buildings or houses, only the thousands of lit windows from the great skyscrapers and the impressive signs with words and names in gas flames. Hundreds of steamboats swarm around our ship. They are built peculiarly, very tall with many windows that are also lit up this evening. Because of the darkness, we really cannot see much of the people on the ferries, only their illuminated windows, which gives an even more impressive effect. Slowly we finally glide into our appointed dock; and our trip on the great, stormy ocean is finished. First, second, and those American citizens in third class are the first to go ashore; but we poor third-class immigrants have much to go through before we receive our freedom. We must spend another night on board.

℘)ෆ

November 1:   Around 9 o'clock we get to go ashore and arrive at a large baggage area. There we see all of our beautiful trunks, which have been unloaded during the night. For the first time we set our feet on American soil. Now the customs officials come to inspect our baggage and trunks. It is a real bother to have to open all of our trunks that are so well secured with ropes. The women have a hard time, and we have to help them. The actual inspection is not very thorough. One could smuggle as much as one wanted; all one would have to do is put the contraband in the middle of the trunk, because they only pull up the corners. I had with me several silver items that belonged to my sister, but they did not see them. Otherwise I probably would have had to pay a tariff. After this procedure, something was written in chalk on the things that had been inspected. Now the trunks were to be sent to their places of destination. Their large amount made a lot of noise when they were removed.

I have gotten too far, however, into the story. We were, you see, brought out on a ferry, trunks and all, to a place that is called Ellis Island to undergo a lot of things. It was very cold that morning, and a light fog hung over the city. We stood there packed in like sardines, about 800 on the same ferry; and then we were off to the island. There we had to go into a building and wait in an orderly line. I do not remember what it was called. Then we came to a large area with many gratings and hallways. We had to pass through all of those hallways, so we began doing so. First we came to a doctor to be inspected once more; and if we passed, we could continue. At the end of each hallway there was a desk, and a man sat there writing with an interpreter at his side. We

FIGURE 8.1   View of Ellis Island, N.Y., looking across the water toward immigration station. Photograph taken in 1913. (Library of Congress, Prints & Photographs Division LC-USZ62-40101)

were arranged so that the Swedes were in one corridor, the Englishmen in another, the French in another, and so on. When I stood before Pontius Pilate, he asked me where I was going, if I had any relatives or friends who would receive me, what I was going to do in this country, and how much money I had with me. Since I answered all of the questions satisfactorily, I was allowed to continue; and I now came to the ticket office, where I had to show proof that I had paid for my entire ticket already in Göteborg. Then I got my railroad ticket consisting of six different parts, which meant—if I remember correctly—that I would be traveling on this many trains.

Then came the inspection that I mentioned previously. My trunk was too heavy, so I had to pay $3.75 for the additional weight. That amounts to about 14 Swedish crowns. Then I was led to the waiting room for my train. That was the first time I can say that I ever sat in jail; how the time passed slowly, but I endured it. In the evening, several emigrants came from another boat. They were Italians, I believe. All of my friends got to leave before me. Only two or three of them had to wait as long as I did; but they were not going on the same train, so I would not have their company. The largest part of the noisy, dirty Italians was to constitute my pleasant traveling companions. At 8 o'clock we were finally put on a ferry that took us to our various stations. What a racket there was on that ferry, where we were standing almost on top of one another. The Italians smoked, shrieked, fought among themselves, played their accordions—and they smelled repulsive. Then I said good-bye to my three friends and arrived at my station. I had to wait there until 9 o'clock until the train was finally ready to receive us, and at last the difficulties of New York had ended.

℘℘℘

November 2:   I have now spent my first night on an American train. It went well. The cars are unusually long and wide with two rows of seats and one in the middle. The seats are upholstered with plush covers and arranged so that they can be inclined, so we were almost able to be lying horizontally if we wanted. That is good for the night. It is altogether too nice for the dirty Italians, who have all of their baggage with them and spit everywhere. I was shown to a special place. Gradually one emigrant after another gets off the train, and soon there are not more than three of us left, namely, a Russian, a Serbian girl, and me.

The train rushes through very beautiful countryside with low, wooded hills and occasionally one sees pleasant little villas of an unusual style. The train, which is an emigrant train, does not go particularly fast and stops often. Now and then, however, it does accelerate; but I thought that it might be worse. The telegraph poles are like small staffs and, believe me, they are not straight or beautiful as in Sweden, but rather crooked and leaning in all directions. The fields in the countryside seem to be unusually well taken care of. Almost everything is done by machine here.

We pass through several large towns, and everywhere we see streetcars. Among them, we pass through the one that Prince Wilhelm visited last summer—Jamestown. But since only a short stop was made there, we did not have the opportunity to see the exposition that was still taking place. We were able to glimpse it hastily from the train. Among other things, I saw a very large wheel with cages that people could enter and ride up into the air. Toward afternoon a lot of American youngsters came into our compartment. They were unusually loud and descended on us foreigners, wanting to talk with us. Of special interest to them was the Serbian girl, who was dressed in her national costume. They gave her apples, oranges, and bananas. She was rather pretty. I was invited by them to have coffee and sandwiches. We had moved to another car. Since it would soon be time to go to bed, one of the Americans was going to show me how to change the seat. It was a different kind, where one could completely stretch out with one's clothes on. He almost crushed the top of his right index finger. Now it was time to sleep, but I did not get very much.

All Americans were not as friendly as these; some were just the opposite. I entered a car where there was a lot of room; but they drove me out, saying that they were clean Americans and did not want any foreigners near them. Since I could not express myself in their language as I wanted to, I had to leave.

℘)℘

November 3:   Well, I have slept another night on an American train. It is now 6:30 a.m. In a few hours we shall be in Chicago, the great city that has received so many Swedes. In this part of the country there are large cornfields. It looks as if the ears have been cut off with only the stalks remaining. Even they have been cut down in many places and set out to dry. I hardly ever see any churches, but occasionally there is a little chapel. Cemeteries enclosed by fences are scattered here and there in the countryside. The houses are of wood, and often they have two floors.

Now at 11:00 o'clock we are arriving in Chicago, but it takes a while before we are ready to stop at our station. When I found out that I had to stay here until 6 o'clock p.m., I quickly decided to go out on the town to see the sights. The tall buildings surprised me. The tallest one that I saw was twenty stories, but even taller ones do exist. In New York they are building one with forty stories for the Singer Sewing Machine Company. I even went to a museum. I traveled several miles on a streetcar and went to the city's largest cemetery. Such expensive monuments they have there and what grounds! But I must hurry to see what I want to, since it is almost 6 o'clock. Because it is Sunday, it is unusually quiet in the city. I lost my way once, but then I unexpectedly encountered some of my friends from the boat. They had come on another train, and with their help I found the station.

Soon I was on another train belonging to the Santa Fe Railroad. This one was even more comfortable than the previous one. I was now on a friendly passenger train and had the opportunity to see many *different* types of Americans. Most of the help on the train are Negroes. The conductor is white. He has an assistant who helps and directs the passengers on and off the train, lights the lamps, and so forth. The conductor has only to check the tickets. But now I have to go to sleep. Good night.

℘)℘

November 4:   Now it is morning. I slept well last night. The weather is nice, and I feel very fine. People come and go continually; and I have the opportunity to see all types, including many Negroes. Without exception the women are very elegant, even the Negro women. The day passes and we continue on our journey west. . . . Now I have to stop writing for a while. We are coming to Kansas City, and there I am supposed to change trains.

Now I am out on an unpleasant adventure. I asked one of the stewards if I should get off at the station we came to; he said that I should not. I stayed on, thinking that I would get off at another station in the same city. Then the conductor came to check our tickets. When he got to me, he scratched his head and said that I was on the wrong train and bawled out the steward, who had been wrong, and told him to help me off at the next stop. We came to a station called Kallidog, and there I did get off. I was afraid that my ticket would be void if I did not get back for the next train, but the agent told me that there was no danger. I was to go back with a train that was to come at 3 o'clock p.m. It was now 11 o'clock a.m., and my train in Kansas City was not supposed to leave until 6 o'clock p.m. So if I had gotten off in Kansas City, I would have had to wait there the whole time. When I heard this I thought that I had not lost much, since I got to make this trip. It did not cost anything, either. I did some scouting in the area. It was very lovely with thick forests. A large park with oak trees was nearby, there were many fine houses, and near the trees was a large cornfield. It was warm that day, like a June day in Sweden. Here the leaves had not fallen off as much as they already had to the east. I went to a lunchroom and got something to eat. I also went to a store and bought some paper, envelopes, and stamps and wrote a letter to Papa, sitting on a bench outside. It was an unusually calm and peaceful place in the noisy country, America.

I wished that I could stay there for a while; but it was soon 3 o'clock and I had to leave, thus ending my adventure. In Kansas City I had to wait for almost two hours, but they passed quickly. The waiting room was comfortable and pleasant, furnished with rocking chairs, too, if one wanted to use them. Since it was dark, there was no point in going out on the town; I only went out to eat. Now I was half way to my destination, I only had about 2,000 American miles left. At 6 o'clock I got on the Missouri Pacific train and soon was headed for unknown parts. A steward offered me a pillow that I gratefully accepted; but then he wanted 25 cents, about 90 *öre,* so there was not much to thank him for. I soon went to sleep.

℘৩ⳤ

November 5:   This train's third-class section is also very nice and comfortable. It is more pleasant to be on a friendly passenger train than on the dirty emigrant one . . .

Occasionally we pass a town, but not the kind we have in Sweden. These places are, on the other hand, villages with a few small, run-down houses; and instead of water pipes, there is a windmill near every house. About midday we go through a place called Pueblo. All kinds of people were there. One saw Mexicans wearing large hats that resembled beehives, with unusually large brims. There were also Chinese, Japanese, and a lot of cowboys from the nearby prairie. I was supposed to change trains there. I did not have to wait more than half an hour . . .

ᏸᎧᏇ

November 6:   When the train comes to a stop, I wake up. It is reported that an engine is broken. Nothing unusual on American trains. After two hours we are finally ready for departure, and we now pass through interesting county. On all sides we are surrounded by unusually high mountains. The peaks are snow covered; and on their northern sides, the snow extends even further down. In spite of their mountainous area, there are not many tunnels; but we do go through a few. One of them took almost fifteen minutes. We travel up the mountains instead of going through them. In order to gain altitude, the train cannot go straight up; but rather it has to traverse zig-zags, which makes the trip doubly long.

Up on the mountains the view is marvelous. There are even more mountain ranges, the snow-covered peaks of which glitter in the sun. The mountains contain many precious metals, including gold. They are mostly bare, but occasionally one sees pine trees. The telegraph poles are of iron, and some of them have fallen down here. Between the ridges are fertile valleys where other trains can be seen. They look more like toys, at least from our perspective. The railroad we see down there is the same one on which we are traveling. Are we going down there? No, it seems impossible. But in a little while—a half hour or so—we have wound our way down there; and we now rush forward through a lovely valley with summer weather and farms that have fruit bearing trees, especially apples. We travel through this area the rest of the day, passing by towns now and then. I shall not arrive today either, they say, but rather must change trains once more. I am beginning to get tired.

In the afternoon we arrived at a place called Grand Junction, where I was to change trains. My new train would not be leaving until 2:30 a.m., so I went out into the town. The street illumination in American towns, however, is poor; and the danger is great. I then went into the waiting room for men; and because I was tired, I out my bag under my head and a paper under my feet. I thought that I would sleep a little bit; but soon an employee made me get up, saying that sleeping was not permitted here. Several others had followed my example, and they were told to get up. Then I got thirsty, but there was no water in the men's drinking fountain. So I took a paper cup and went to the ladies' waiting room. There were not any women there, so I dared to go in. But then the same employee came and told me to leave. That is the way emigrants are treated in the land of the free.

ᏸᎧᏇ

November 7:   It was finally 2:30 p.m. and my train had arrived, and I was glad to be on my way again. When I boarded the train, the conductor told me to get off because there was no room. I had to wait for the next train. It was also uncertain if I could get on that one. According to the timetable it was supposed to leave at 4:30; but as that half hour drew near, a station master came and wrote on a board that the train was late and would not arrive until 5:30. At 5:30 no train appeared. It eventually came at 6:30.

Now at 8 o'clock we finally are leaving this mudhole of a town after having waited for fourteen hours. They are very punctual here. I have now gotten on another emigrant train; and almost all of the passengers are filthy, dark Italians who are going to San Francisco. They make a lot of noise, splash their dirty wine in the drinking water, and so forth. The area we are passing is flat and then mountainous. On the plains only fruit seems to be cultivated. Thousands of trees have been planted in straight lines, and they look well taken care of. For the most part, the fruit has already been picked; but now and then one can see a tree filled with large, red apples. I have been told that the fruit crop was bad this year.

After traveling for several hours, we see a mountain wall, a vertical stretch. To the east is Colorado, and to the west lies Utah. I am now in the state where I am going to stay for some time. The day passes as usual, and at 8 o'clock p.m. we finally reach Salt Lake City, the goal of my journey. Three weeks ago to the day, I left Sweden. After I had asked a policeman for directions, I got to the home of my dear ones here about 9 o'clock and surprised them before they were ready for bed.

Thank you, dear God, for everything—for Your protection during my long journey.

In the Classroom

Chronological Thinking

- Construct a time line of significant events in the history of immigration to the United States.
- Identify how Swensson's attitude toward his journey changed by citing specific passages and evidence in his diary.

Historical Comprehension

- Write a narrative describing the Ellis Island experience.
- Trace Swensson's route using a world map and calculate the total distance he traveled.

Historical Analysis and Interpretation

- Infer what U.S. society would look like today had the country closed its doors to immigrants.
- Examine the arguments against immigration.

Historical Research Capabilities

- Potential Topics:
  Swedish Immigration   Ellis Island
  RMS *Adriatic*   Immigration from other countries

Historical Issues-Analysis and Decision-Making

- Identify the major reasons people immigrated to the United States.
- Describe the contributions made by immigrants to U.S. culture, science, the arts, literature, and politics.

9

World War I: Dear Sergeant Armstrong

Miss Walker read the letter aloud. Perhaps at an assembly of students and teachers in the school auditorium, at a "Support Our Boys" rally outside on the school grounds, or simply to a small group of students in a history class. Although we do not know when or under what circumstances the letter was read to the students of Indianapolis Public School #17, we can imagine they listened with great interest, curiosity, and pride to the words written by a popular history teacher who was serving his country overseas in World War I.

The letters in this chapter were written by junior high school students in response to a letter from Irven Armstrong, the former history teacher serving in the U.S. Army in France. They were likely part of a class assignment, because they were all written on the same date, November 7, 1918.

Irven Armstrong's letter unfortunately no longer exists. Its content, however, can be partially reconstructed based on the student responses. He reported his promotion to Sergeant ("I am very glad you have been promoted to Sergeant"), described some of the sights he had seen while overseas ("I was very glad to hear from you and to hear of the interesting places that you have seen"), and conveyed his general well-being ("We were glad to know that you were getting along nicely").

The ten student letters give us a glimpse of life on the home front during World War I and reflect the tremendous wave of patriotic fervor sweeping the nation in the fall of 1918. While they are clearly proud of Sergeant Armstrong's contribution to the war effort ("We, as pupils of School No. 17 were very glad to hear from you and to know that you are in France helping to make the world safe for democracy"), the students appear to take even greater pride in describing their own efforts to assist "the men and boys over there." "Our parents are buying Liberty bonds, we are buying Thrift Stamps and War Savings Stamps. We are also saving the pits of fruit and nuts in order to furnish carbon for the gas masks."

The letters to Sergeant Armstrong also expose, however, an aspect of U.S. life of which we can take less pride. Irven Armstrong was an African American, the son of a former slave. When the United States entered the war in April 1917, no black men were allowed in the Marines, Coast Guard, or Air Force. They could serve in the Navy, but only as messmen or kitchen workers. The Army permitted African American volunteers and draftees, but assigned them to segregated units like the 351st Field Artillery, in which Armstrong was a sergeant. One of the students poignantly expresses her hope that Sergeant Armstrong will "get promoted to Lieutenant." Armstrong could have been promoted to Lieutenant, but could rise in rank no further, for in the segregated Army of 1918, no African Americans were able to attain a rank higher than first lieutenant and in no unit could an African American outrank a white officer.

FIGURE 9.1 Seated are Irven Armstrong's parents, Edward and Sarah. Standing behind their parents, all in uniform, are the five Armstrong brothers. From left to right: Charles, Lindzey, Irven, Ezekiel, and Isaac. (Robbins, Coy. (1984). *Black Heritage in Westfield, Indiana,* Bloomington: the author.)

The fall of 1918 also witnessed the peak of the worst epidemic in American history. The number of Americans who died from Spanish Influenza was ten times greater than the number of American soldiers killed in the war. "There has been an epidimic of Influenza here and the schools, churches and all places of amusement were closed for four weeks."

Irven Armstrong was born on March 7, 1892 in Westfield, Indiana. He enrolled in Indiana University in the fall of 1910, but left after one semester to teach at a small school in Hamilton County. His teaching salary was needed to assist his parents and to help pay for his college education. Armstrong re-enrolled in the fall of 1911 and graduated with a degree in history in 1915. He was the first initiate of Kappa Alpha Psi, the first African American fraternity in the United States. Armstrong's four brothers, Isaac, Ezekial, Charles, and Lindzey served in World War I, as well.

Armstrong earned a master's degree from Butler University after the war and continued his career as a history teacher, retiring from Crispus Attucks High School in Indianapolis in 1959. Irven Armstrong died on May 10, 1996. He was 104 years old.

ℰ Letters to Sergeant Armstrong ℛ

Indianapolis, Ind.,
Nov. 7, 1918

Dear Sergeant Armstrong,

I hope you can come back and see seventeen once more. We are making another great drive for Thrift Stamps.

School has been closed for four weeks on the account of the Epedimic called "Spanish Enfluenza. I was very sorry school closed, but, I would much rather stay at home than to come to school while the Epedimic was raging.

I would like to see France and its inhabitants. I always did think it was a beautiful country, because I studied France when I was seventh "B". In October I visited the War Exhibits. Some of the shells were very prodigious. I saw the german's helmets. I saw the French shells and bullet and other interesting things.

I am very glad you have been promoted to Sergeant and I hope you will get promoted to Lieutenant.

Yours sincerely,

ℰℛ

Irven Armstrong (1892–1996) Collection, 1918–1996, Collection #M 0745, Indiana Historical Society.

Indianapolis, Ind;
Nov. 7, 1918

Dear friend,

Your letter was very interesting, we were all glad to know you were getting along so nicely. We are all doing our bit toward helping the men and boys over there.

The "Fourth Liberty Loan Drive" is on now. Since I am not able to buy a "Bond" I am buying Thrift Stamps. Some of my relatives are buying both Liberty Bonds and Thrift Stamps.

I am willing to (soar) sacrifice a little food and many over here, because the men and boys are sacrificing there lives that we may have better privileges and have Democracy and not Autocracy.

We have been out of school on account of a dreadful deasease called Spanish inflaunza. We were out of school for five weeks and all other public places were closed for the same Amount of time. We have been back in school nearly a week so you can imagine how far behind ~~were~~ we are in our studies.

I hope you will continue to have success and will return soon.

Yours Sincerely,

FIGURE 9.2 Remember Belgium. Fourth Liberty Loan poster depicts a German soldier wearing a pointed helmet leading a girl by the hand with a city burning in the background. (Library of Congress, Prints & Photographs Division, LC-USZ62-19905)

శు)ఇ

Indianapolis, Ind.,
Nov. 7, 1918.

Dear Mr. Armstrong,

I was very glad to hear from you and to hear of the interesting places that you have seen.

Now I will try to tell you of some of the things that we are doing. We are still buying Thrift Stamps. We are bringing peach seeds, apricot seeds and plum seeds to school.

This is for carbon, to make gas masks for the soldiers. We are trying to do our bit.

The fourth Liberty Loan Bond is out now. Every one is being urged to buy one. The purpose of this bond is to help the soldiers during the winter.

Sincerely yours,

శు)ఇ

Indianapolis, Ind.,
November 7, 1918.

Dear Sergeant Armstrong,

We have had nearly four weeks vacation from school. It has been a contagious disease here known as, the "Spanish Influenza". Several people died of it.

We had a great Liberty Loan drive during the month of October, and it was successful. All the counties in Indiana had reach their quota at the end of the drive. A great deal of them had over- their quota.

I am doing well at school. I am now in the eight B (8th B) grade. We miss you very much at school. We are also glad to know you are thinkink of old seventeen, and will be delighted to hear from you any time.

Election day was here on the fifth of this month. Indiana is Republic. I remain,

Your sincerely pupil,

శు)ఇ

Indianapolis, Ind.,
Nov. 7, 1918

Dear Mr. Armstrong,

We were especially glad to hear from you and also glad to get your interesting letter read to us.

We are very proud to hear of your rapid advancement and it makes us feel proud to think that you are from dear old Seventeen.

The Influenza Epedemic has kept us out of school for about three or four weeks but we have now returned and are working with might and main to make up those four weeks.

Indiana has gone "over the top" in the great fourth Liberty Loan the folks back at home are doing every thing available to boost those who are sacrificing their lives for them over the top.

Yours Sincerely,

℘⋙⋘

Indianapolis, Ind.,
Nov. 7, 1918.

Dear Sergeant Armstrong,

We received your interesting letter a few days ago and was very glad to hear from you. We were glad to know that you were getting along nicely. Your letter was very interesting to me. France must be a very beautiful place. I should like to be there on a visit myself.

We are all doing our bit here by buying Thrift Stamps to help the soldiers that are sacrificing their lives for democracy. Our school is still one hundred percent in Thrift Stamp buyers. I hope it will stay that way. One girl from our school was a Field Marshall in buying and selling Thrift Stamps. There are others hoping to be high officers of that sort by and by.

We miss you much since you left us last year. It seems that their is no one that can fill your place. I cant thing more at present to tell you. Write when ever you have time for we are always ready to hear from you and glad too. From a pupil.

℘⋙⋘

Indianapolis, Ind.,
Nov. 7, 1918.

Dear Sergeant Armstrong,

We, as pupils of School No. 17 were very glad to hear from you and to know that you are in France, helping to make the world safe for democracy. You soldiers are not the only one's fighting for this cause, but we here in America are backing you and thousands of other soldiers and officers. One proof for this is that a fourth Liberty Loan drive was started the twenty-eighth of September and lasted until October the nineteenth. Of course Marion County went

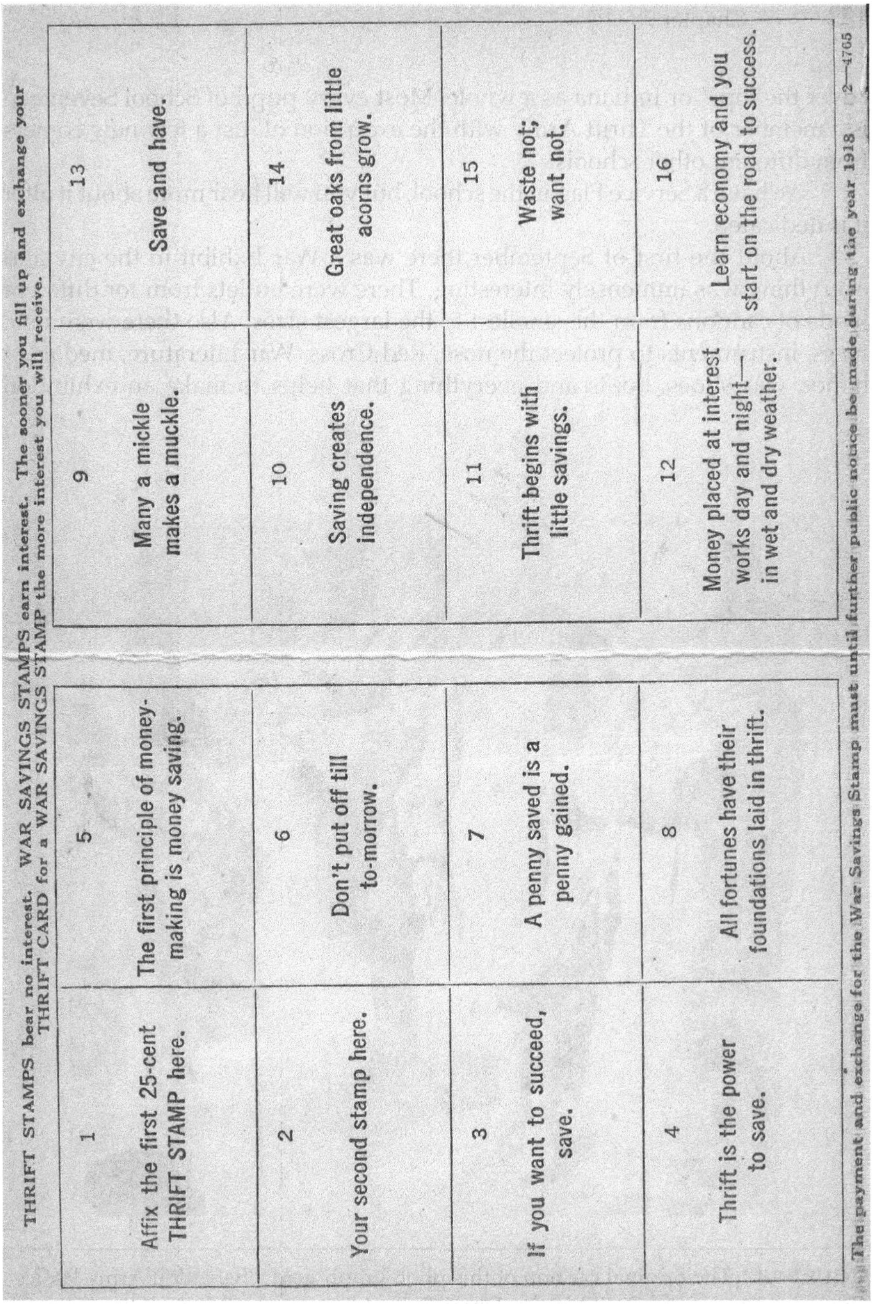

THRIFT STAMPS bear no interest. WAR SAVINGS STAMPS earn interest. The sooner you fill up and exchange your THRIFT CARD for a WAR SAVINGS STAMP the more interest you will receive.

1 — Affix the first 25-cent THRIFT STAMP here.

2 — Your second stamp here.

3 — If you want to succeed, save.

4 — Thrift is the power to save.

5 — The first principle of money-making is money saving.

6 — Don't put off till to-morrow.

7 — A penny saved is a penny gained.

8 — All fortunes have their foundations laid in thrift.

9 — Many a mickle makes a muckle.

10 — Saving creates independence.

11 — Thrift begins with little savings.

12 — Money placed at interest works day and night— in wet and dry weather.

13 — Save and have.

14 — Great oaks from little acorns grow.

15 — Waste not; want not.

16 — Learn economy and you start on the road to success.

The payment and exchange for the War Savings Stamp must until further public notice be made during the year 1918

2—4765

FIGURE 9.3 Interior view of a U.S. Government Thrift Card. Once the card was filled with 25-cent Thrift Stamps, a War Savings Certificate would be issued. This could be redeemed at a later date for $5.00. (United States Government Thrift Card, interior view. 1918 issue (WS 1A). 10.9 × 15.2 cm (opened). Courtesy of the Massachusetts Historical Society) "over the top," or Indiana as a whole. Most every pupil of School Seventeen is a member of the Thrift Army with the exception of just a few new comers from different other schools.

We have a Service Flag in the school, but you will hear more about it after it is dedicated.

About the first of September there was a War Exhibit in the city and everything was immensely interesting. There were bullets from for different kinds of cannons from the smallest to the largest sizes. Also there were time fuses, instruments to protect the nose, Red Cross, War Literature, medals of honor, war shoes, boots and everything that helps to make an exhibition

FIGURE 9.4   The original caption of this photograph read: "Salvation Army lassies giving sweets to returned [African American] soldiers. Two soldiers of the 351st Field Artillery which returned on the 'Louisville' receiving candy from the Salvation Army Lassies that welcome every troopship that comes to port at all times and in all kinds of weather." Irven Armstrong served in the 351st Field Artillery. (ARC Identifier 533625, Variant Control Number NWDNS-165-WW-127(133), National Archives and Records Administration, College Park, MD)

worthwhile. There are many other letters being written to you so I will not make mine too lengthy. Will close for this time.

Yours truly,

ৎ)承

Indianapolis, Ind.,
Nov. 7, 1918.

Dear Mr. Armstrong,

While being in Chicago I went to the War Exposition to see articles that were used in battle. The helmets, swords and things like that were not very interesting. The thing that interesed me most was the statue of liberty and the sham battle.

I wasn't here when you went away, therefor I was very much surprised when I found you were gone. When I went to Chicago three years ago I told mother that I wished I had a stayed so I could have been in your room. Do you remember I had justed passed in to the six A, I was in your room just one day. "Do you remember me?"

In Chicago I bought thrift stamps. I have one War Saving Stamp and four thrift stamps, the money of which I saved my ownself. Since I have been in Indianapolis I haven't bought any because all the spare money goes for books. I am in the eighth grade now, so you see every penny I get goes for books because the more I put off getting them the further I am thrown back. But after I get all fixed with my books and lessons, I will help back you up by buying more thrift stamps. I am going to help up put you and Pershing some where in Germany instead of somewhere in France.

Yours sincerely

ৎ)承

Indianapolis, Ind.
Nov. 7, 1918

Sergeant Armstrong,

I am a pupil of No. 17 School. My name is _____. You were at one time my Mathematics teacher. The letter you wrote to the pupils of this school was received. I enjoyed listening to it being read to us by Miss Walker. All of the school children are doing all they can to help the men and boys who have gone Over There. We still have our Air Plane races and each child does all he can to see that his room gets in the lead. We are bringing peach seeds to school to be used in making carbon for gas masks. A Liberty Loan drive began here

Oct. 28th and from the way the papers read the colored people did their bit. We children are buying Thrift Stamps and War Stamps. The teachers still give us our buttons to show where we rank in the Thrift Army. I am corporal now but by the time this letter reaches you I hope to be Sergt.

There has been an epidimic of Influenza here and the schools, churches and all places of amusement were closed for four weeks. During the last week fewer cases were reported so everything opened again and we are back in school. I was a victim of the Influenza but I am alright now.

Yours sincerely,

ℰℭ

Indianapolis, Ind.,
Nov. 7, 1918

Dear Sergeant Armstrong,

We were delighted to hear from you. We are doing everything to help win the war. Our parents are buying Liberty Bonds, we are buying Thrift Stamps and War Savings Stamps. We are also saving the pits of fruit and nuts in order to furnish carbon for the gas masks. It takes I think two hundred seeds (for) to make carbon for one gas mask so we have to have a great number of them to get carbon for at least twenty gas masks.

I wasn't one of your pupils but I know they all miss you because I know I do.

Yours Sincerely,

*In the Classroom*_____

Chronological Thinking

- Develop a time line of the significant events of World War I.
- Identify the significant events in the efforts to desegregate the United States military.

Historical Comprehension

- Write a narrative describing life on the home front in the United States during World War I.
- Describe the three most important things students wanted to communicate to Sergeant Armstrong.

Historical Analysis and Interpretation

- Design a Liberty Bond or Thrift Stamp poster.
- Reconstruct Irven Armstrong's letter using the letters by students and additional historical research.

FIGURE 9.5 At the age of 94, Irven Armstrong appeared on the cover of the 75th anniversary issue of the *Kappa Alpha Psi Journal.* (Courtesy of Kappa Alpha Psi)

Historical Research Capabilities

- Potential Topics:

World War I	African Americans in the U.S. military
Spanish Influenza	Liberty Bonds
Thrift Stamps	Kappa Alpha Psi fraternity

Historical Issues-Analysis and Decision-Making

- Analyze how the attitudes held by the students regarding U.S. participation in World War I had an impact on their actions.

- Write a letter to President Woodrow Wilson in which you present a case for the desegregation of the United States military.

10

The Great Depression: Letters to Mrs. Roosevelt

In the spring of 1935, a young girl from Salida, Colorado sat down and wrote the wife of the President of the United States asking her for money. "I was just wondering, if you could do something, so I can graduate from the Eight grade. It will take about $10.00. . . . I read a lot a about you in the papers we get from the neighbors." Eleanor Roosevelt, as no other first lady had before her, connected with ordinary Americans, especially young people. During the worst economic crisis in this nation's history, they wrote to her in unprecedented numbers, sending 300,000 letters alone during her first year in Washington.

Officially beginning with the stock market crash on Black Tuesday, October 29, 1929, the Great Depression lasted nearly ten years. Children went without food, clothing, and birthday and Christmas gifts as mothers and fathers lost their jobs and thus their sources of income. Letters the young correspondents wrote to Mrs. Roosevelt describe their circumstances and allow us a rare perspective on the effects that this period had on its youngest victims and their lives.

"[M]y father was layed off after working for the railroad fifteen years." Unemployment in 1929 was 3.2 percent. Four years later it had increased to nearly 25 percent. The needy were forced to rely upon churches and private charities for assistance because the federal government had no social agencies or welfare programs. Until 1933, the government did little to assist the needy, standing firm in its belief that the economy would recover on its own.

"[M]y father does not earn enough on the C.W.A." "I'm writing you in regard to this W.P.A. work which my Father works on." "The N.R.A. is coming along fine." Inaugurated in March of 1933, Franklin

Delano Roosevelt brought a new philosophy to the White House, and in the first one hundred days of his administration he signed legislation that established many of what became known as the "alphabet agencies." Their primary goal was to get people back to work and put money in their pockets. "[M]y father just started on to work in one of those job your good Husband started for the poor people and we were sure glad to see him working as he did not work in year he is only makeing $15 a week. But thank God he is getting that."

The National Youth Administration (NYA) was one alphabet agency designed specifically to assist unemployed high school and college students in continuing their education. "On this NYA job I get $18.48 a mo . . . I have had 2½ yrs, of experience in this line of work under the NYA. First two years was while I was in high school." During the course of its existence, the NYA employed over two million students in part-time jobs.

The Great Depression impacted farm families in the American Midwest particularly hard. "I am in the dust bowl. We didn't raise any crop this year. And we have to live off of the releif and theres no injoyment out of that." Many were unable to meet mortgage payments when food prices dropped precipitously early in the depression. A bushel of wheat that sold for three dollars in 1920 brought only thirty cents in 1932. Thousands of farmers lost their farms when banks foreclosed on their mortgages. When it seemed it could not get any worse, a series of droughts beginning in 1933 created vast dust storms that blanketed large portions of the country.

Many of the letter writers to Mrs. Roosevelt requested clothing, gifts, cars, and money because poverty was so far-reaching and pervasive during the decade of the 1930s. "I am here to ask you for $8.00 to get me a winter coat." "[I]f your little grandchildren have any little things from last year I will be thankful to see you send them to us." "I am writing to you to see if you will buy me a new car or pickup"; "*If you help me go to college Mrs. Roosevelt, I will work and pay you back.*"

Receiving over 800 letters a day, Mrs. Roosevelt could not read or personally reply to all of them. Her staff set aside about fifty letters for the First Lady to read each day and, of those, she responded to only a few. The great majority of young letter writers actually received a form letter signed by one of Mrs. Roosevelt's secretaries informing them that their requests for assistance were denied.

Eleanor Roosevelt spent her life, both during and after her tenure as First Lady, championing assistance for the poor, the homeless, and the helpless. That these desperate, sincere cries for help from her fellow Americans had to be denied must have greatly tormented her.

FIGURE 10.1 Eleanor Roosevelt at White Top Mountain, Virginia, August 12, 1933. (Courtesy of the Franklin D. Roosevelt Presidential Library, Digital archives)

ℬ *Letters to Mrs. Roosevelt* ℛ

Brownsville, Penn.
May 25, 1934

Honorable Mrs. Roosevelt,

My uncle has been telling me of the help you have been giving to the miners and their family's and I am a miners daughter. Age 18. I never finished school Because I was ill. My heart was bad. It has been well for the past two years. But I cant afford to go to school as my father is unable to work But draws a government pension which is enough to support us but as we have a large family it is not enough to dress us. I have earned my tuition for Business College working for a lady in our town. I visited a girls club in California and one of the Subjects was the Description of the White House and it was said the attic of the White House was over flowing with discarded clothing if this is true and

Eleanor Roosevelt Papers, Material Assistance Requested files, Franklin D. Roosevelt Presidential Library and Museum, Hyde Park, New York.

you would send me some I am rather . . . clever with a needle and I would be forever grateful

   A. E.

℘Ↄ〣

Barboursville, W. Va.
August, 23, 1934

Dear President & Wife;

This is the first time I or Any of my people wrote Any president. And I am here to ask you for $8.00 to get me a winter coat. This may seem very strange for a girl 12 years old to do but my father is a poor honest working Laundry man and he works on a percentage a week we have 10 in our family and my father does not have enough money to get him a bottle of Beer. He is a democrat and did all he could to have you voted. The N.R.A. [National Recovery Administration] is coming along fine. As little as I am I know just as much about depression as a grown person. I'm 12 years old and am in the 8th grade curly hair Brunette & brown eyes & fair complexion & weigh 76 lbs. Hoping to hear from you soon I remain your true Democrat

   J. A. G.

P.S. We would have loved if Mrs. Roosevelt when she was visiting Logan to come around to our small town she was only about 60 miles from here.

℘Ↄ〣

Birmingham, Ala.
July 27, 1938

Dear Mrs. Roosevelt.

I'm writing you in regard to this W.P.A. work which my Father works on. He did make $36 per month but I think he will get a raise of $4.80 on the month But he has five to support Three children and I'm the oldest one fifteen years of age but to young to hold a job. I can't go to Church or Sunday school any more for the need of clothes.

   Mother and daddy dont go either because their clothes are to bad.

   If you have any clothes that you dont want mother can make them fit us. Please Mrs. Roosevelt dont mention this over the radio or in the papers. my school mates would nag me to death. but if you think its false call or write Relief Headquarters Birmingham.

   Thanking you I am

FIGURE 10.2   WPA (Works Progress Administration) worker and family at dinner. Zeigler, Illinois, January 1939. (Library of Congress, Prints & Photographs Division, LC-USF34-026736-D DLC)

ॐ

Salida Colo.
May 7–1935

Dear Mrs. Roosevelt,

I was just wondering, if you could do something, so I can graduate from the Eight grade. It will take about $10.00 and then I got to make my confirmation and there is three of my other brothers, too, and one sister, beside me. The work relief don't do right here, they give those girls in the relief office $20 a week, and they only support theirself and they give a man with, a family of seven, $48.00 a month, last month they gave us $46.00, when he should get $58 at the least. How much do you think a family of seven should get? Mother hadn't no light, now because we didn't have enough money to paid for them . . . and we are way far back in rent. Some men here get $6.00 a day, and they only got two or three in a family, because they are the boss or timekeeper. I think if Mr. Roosevelt get the old-age Pension [i.e. Social Security] in it will be a lot better than the relief work. Every week we go to bed one or two days without anything to eat. My brother and I go down to the railroad track to pick up coal to keep warm. If only the Railroad Pension go through daddy will have steady work on the railroad. We hardly get enough to wear, we have to wash out our clothes and put them back on. Gosh! Mother can't get a hair-cut, her hair looked terrible.

If the Old Age Pension go in these girls got to go out and do something else, beside working on the relief. Gosh! I used to be able to take care of baby but now the big girls get the job, we used to only get .10 cent, to take care of a little girl, but the girls, that take care of her, now get .50 a day and .50 cents a night. I read a lot a about you in the papers we get from the neighbors. My mother and Dad don't know I am writing to you. Please answer as soon as possible. Gosh! May 15th we have to try to make our confirmation if we can get some clothes and a dollar each too. I hope mother or dad wont find out I writing to you, because they don't want to let anyone, know how hard-up we are.

Please Please write immediately. I heard you help the poor peoples. I wish God blessed you, and let you luck. Please answer as soon as you received this letter.

Your's Very Truly,
Miss A. M.

℘℧

Nov. 30, 1937
Springfield Mass

Dear Mrs. Roosevelt:

I am a girl sixteen years old. Last May I beg my father to buy an electric re-frigerator for mother on mother's day. We had talked about buying one with her. She thought it was not a very wise thing to do, because we could not af-ford to pay cash. I wanted it so very bad that my father bought it. He agreed to pay monthly payments of seven dollars and twenty two cents. What mother had sayed proved to be right. For two weeks after we bought the re-frigerator I took sick with a serious kidney ailment which confined me to my bed from May twenty until Nov. twenty-second. I am just recovering from a delicate operation. I came home from the hospital Nov. eighth and my father was layed off after working for the railroad fifteen years. Many a girl of my age is hoping that on Christmas morn they will find a wrist watch, a hand-bag, or even a fur coat. But my one and only wish is to have father and mother spend a happy Christmas Mrs. Roosevelt I am asking of you a favor which can make this wish come true. I am asking you to keep up our payments until my father get's back to work as a Christmas gift to me. Though father worked part time for quite a while we never lost anything for the lack of payments. If the refrigerator was taken away from us father and mother would think it a disgrace.

I close hoping with all my heart that my letter will be consider.

Mrs. Roosevelt you may rest assure that I have learnt my lesson

I am respectfully yours
J. B.

℘℘℘

Denver, Colo.
9-11-41

Dear Mrs. Roosevelt,

Mother and I are grieved so much about daddy that I am writing you to see if you will so good and kind to help us a little so we can see daddy one more time our in come is four dollars and fifty cents a week so you see we can't do much.

My daddy went away one day to look for work. He was killed in Reno Nevada by a Southern Pacific freight train Aug. the 11th was burried Aug. the 18th. Mother and I didn't get the word until Aug. the 22nd. We didn't get to see daddy. They didn't know daddy had mother and I. So they burried daddy in Reno Nevada. We are almost dead with grief. We can't sleep or eat very much. The undertaker there wrote us we could see daddy. They would open the grave for us to see daddy for the last time. but the cost will be fifty dollars and we have'nt the money to pay. Mother cries all the time she said she couldn't live if she couldn't see daddy one more time. It don't seem like daddy is dead daddy was a good man. He and mother loved me. I love my daddy. Mrs. Roosevelt I am asking you with all my heart will you please help us to see my daddy please don't turn us down. I pray to God to help us in the darkest hours of our trouble. You can write to Reno Nevada and you will know this is the truth. I will close for this time praying to hear from you at once with good news. I am a little boy and I go to school every day and I sell pappers after school is out.

A Friend
S. P.

P.S. My daddy's name is A. J. P.

℘℘℘

Brooklyn, New York
May 14, 1934

Dear Mrs. Roosevelt:

I trust you will not misunderstand the writer and please help him out of the rest. I am an admitted freshmen student to the University of Wisconsin but have not enough funds with which to matriculate. I need about two hundred and fifty dollars. Now, I've been reading a great deal of your activities on the radio and heard you on the radio. My parents haven't the money because my father does not earn enough on the C.W.A. [Civil Works Administration] Before he had the position he holds now with the C.W.A. he had a position with a big welfare organization. We had some money saved up for my education. I am ambitious to, and want to study medicine. My father was hurt in an automobile accident about ten months ago and was incapacitated as a result of it. . . . I had a position but the salary was so little I just barely got along on it. . . . Before the C.W.A. job my father had a position and with a little part of each of our earnings we were able to put aside a few dollars. Of course, this entailed a great deal of self denial and scrimping. Recently the old injury was reopened in an unfortunate incident and we paid the doctor some of the money. We don't like charity. I was wondering if you would care to help a young man get started on his educational desire by giving him a helping hand? The proceeds of your money from the radio talks are to be used for education purposes? Why not an Franklin D. Roosevelt scholarship for a needy student? Surely, the President deserves that! Or, better still, and further, why not, as the R.F.C. [Reconstruction Finance Corporation] has loaned money to industry (we construe it as education) an R.F.C. Student Aid Loan Fund as a dedicatory measure to the President of the United States? It can be designated as the Franklin D. Roosevelt Memorial Fund for needy students. Leaving the rest to your discretion and looking forward to spending the year 1934 at the University of Wisconsin,

Yours Very Truly,
L. L.

P.S. I have been in Washington before, but have never seen a President or First Lady. R.S.V.P.

℘℅

[Jersey City, N.J.]
Dec. 14, 1933

Our good Friend Mrs. & Mr. Roosevelt:

Hope this reach you & your good husband Mr. Roosevelt in the best of health. Well Mrs. Roosevelt I am a little girl 12 years old. My mother has 7 small children and my father just started on to work in one of those job your good Husband started for the poor people and we were sure glad to see him working as he did not work in year he is only makeing $15 a week. But thank God he is getting that so my Good Friend you see he will recived he first cheack. Just the time our rent is due so my poor mother will not be able to get my little sisters

& Brother a little doll or a toy for Christmas so if your little grandchildren have any little things from last year I will be thankful to see you send them to us Hope God send you Plenty luck & Health and Hope you have a Happy Christmas & New Year.

C. H.

ഇര

St Paul Minn
Jan 20 1937

Dear Mrs. Lady

Please dont be mad at me for riteing to you. but I have been reding how good you are to every body so I thot maybe you can help me out. my mother ant got no winter coat and it is alful cold here. She works so hard to get us kids clothes and eats that there is nothing left for her so I thot maybe that you having to have new coats for the ineurashion boll and things that you mite have one of your old ones you dont need and you would send it to my ma. I ask Santa Claus to bring her one but there is no such person because she did not get one ples dont tell any one I rote to you as the kids would lafe at me I will have to stop riteing as my ma is comeing home and I dont want her to see this but if you got a coat you dont want I will pray for you all my life no fooling if you make my ma happy it dont have to be so swell just so its warm. I go to the blind school as I cant see very good but mabe somday my eyes will get better. I want you to know that I love you and our president.

Your Friend
D. R.

I am 11 years old only in the 4th grade becaus my eyes are not good. so please excus this Letter

ഇര

Keltner Missouri
January 1, 1938

Dear Mr. & Mrs. Franklin d. Roosevelt:

I am writing to you to see if you will buy me a new car or pick-up. Here is what I want with it. I want to drive to high school. As, for I live in the country where the school busses does not come. They will not come to my home where I live. I am a poor boy and if you will buy me a new pick-up. Then I can earn some of my money to buy some of the gasoline with. If you will buy me a new pick-up it will mean and education to me. If, I had money enough to buy it I wouldn't be writing to you. For you to buy me one. If you will buy me one may be some day I will be president. And if you both are living I will buy you one. If you will buy me one to help get me through high school. For I love school.

I will never forget you if you will buy me one.
I will close.

Yours truly,
O. M.

The kind I want is a Dodge
P.S. I am only fifteen years old.
The pickups cost $677.00
The cars cost $875.00

$$\wp\hspace{-0.5em}\smallsmile\!\!\!\!\smallfrown\hspace{-0.5em}\wp$$

Buffalo, New York
November 11, 1940

Dear Mrs. Roosevelt:

I am a Negro girl 19 years of age who saw your article in the paper relative to what you do with the money you make from writing.

I have been looking for someone to help me out in my problem of higher education. I see, from reading your article, that you have helped some boys and girls go to school through your scholarship fund. I wonder would you consider me as eligible for the next scholarship you give.

My family consists of three children myself included, and also my mother. My mother is a widow and it takes all she can make to feed and cloth us. I have a NYA Job, but do to the fact that my mother is not able to help me I can not go to school. On this NYA job I get $18.48 a mo, the place is located at 243 Washington, Buffalo, N.Y. My work is to take dictation from the head Supervisor and the counselors. I have received many compliments on my work. Some of the girls have received government positions on this job but they have not been able to place any of the Negro girls because they can't find anyone who wants a colored secretary. I feel fully capable of handling any secretarial position. I have had 2½ yrs, of experience in this line of work under the NYA. First two years was while I was in high school the next was at the Personnel Office of the NYA.

Mrs. Roosevelt I have been very despondent over the fact that I have been trying any and every means to go to college, but to no avail. I have competed in oratorical contests in which they offered as first prize a scholarship. The first time I tried I received first place in the state of New York, second time

FIGURE 10.3 Part-time employees of the National Youth Administration personnel office in Illinois, 1936. (Courtesy of the Franklin D. Roosevelt Presidential Library, Digital archives)

2nd in New York, 3rd time 2nd place again at which time I graduated from high school which automatically eliminated me because after you graduate you can no longer compete. I wrote stories, poems, songs, & titles, but only received small prizes, but however I saved this.

What I would like to do Mrs Roosevelt is to go to some school to take business administration to study higher in my secretarial work. I would like to go to Harvard Uni., or the University of Buffalo because these schools offer the complete course. If *you help me go to college Mrs. Roosevelt, I will work and pay you back.*

When I saw your article I thought maybe you would aid me, that is if you consider me worthy, which I hope you will. If you can not help me in my school problem please help me get a job, I am willing to leave the city. I am also willing to work while I go to school. I take 96 words in shorthand, type 50 words a min.

I hope that you will see fit to aid me, I await your speedy answer.

Sincerely
Miss M. C.

ဆၣ

Kismet, Kansas
Nov. 3, 1937

Dear Mrs. Rosevelt:

I am 13 years old and will be 14 the 27 of this month. I am a victim of a shut in. I have been sick ever since the 12 of July. And have a very lonely place to stay. My parence's are very poor people. I cant even go to school yet with the other kids. And doubt if I can this year. I have nothing I can do but set around and I get so lonely I don't know what to do. And if you want to cheer me up and make me one of the happies boys in the world just send me some money

FIGURE 10.4 Dust Storm in Rolla, Kansas, May 6, 1935. The picture was taken from a water tower one hundred feet high. (Courtesy of the Franklin D. Roosevelt Presidential Library, Digital archives)

to get a cheap raido. Ihave got proof by the neighbors that I am sick and have nothing to do. My parence names is Mr. + Mrs. A. J. M. My name is F. M. I live at Kismet. Many, many thanks if you would cheer me up that way I wouldn't spend it for nothing but a radio. It would pass my lonely time a way so much faster. I only ask for a cheep one.

F. M.
Kismet, Kansas

P.S. If I had any thing to do I wouldent ask you of it. It will be highly appreached.

I am in the dust bowl. We didn't raise any crop this year. And we have to live off of the releif and theres no injoyment out of that. But were thankful for it. My mother is sick and under the doctor's care most of the time and my Grandma that lives with me is very poorly. And that keeps my heart broken all the time. And nothing to amuse myself with.

thanks alot

In the Classroom

Chronological Thinking
- Construct a time line of significant events in the Great Depression.
- Examine the letters in chronological order. What conclusions can be drawn?

Historical Comprehension
- Conduct an interview with someone in your family or community who lived through the Great Depression and compare the results of the interview with the content of the letters in this chapter.
- Write a letter to Mrs. Roosevelt from the perspective of a parent of one of the letter writers.

Historical Analysis and Interpretation
- Write a biography of one of the young letter writers.
- Survey a group of students in your school to determine what kinds of things they want but do not possess. Compare that list to the requests of the letter writers in this chapter.

Historical Research Capabilities
- Potential Topics:
  Great Depression   Eleanor Roosevelt
  Franklin Roosevelt   Works Progress Administration
  Dust Bowl

Historical Issues-Analysis and Decision-Making
- Write a letter back to one of the young correspondents offering an alternative solution to their problem.
- Identify the main causes of the Great Depression.

11

Japanese American Internment: Citizens of the Seventh Grade

"Citizens of the Seventh Grade." Historical perspective allows us to look back sixty years and see the irony in that title. The "citizens" of the War Relocation Authority report issued in April 1943 were Mrs. Henderson's seventh grade students at Topaz Junior High School. While they were probably all citizens of the United States, their government had, without due process and any evidence of wrongdoing, forcibly removed them and their families to the high desert in west-central Utah. For a little more than three years, home was the Topaz Relocation Center. In truth, it was a concentration camp and the Japanese American students and their families were prisoners for no other reason than they looked like the "enemy."

Every student of history knows that on December 7, 1941, Japan launched a surprise attack on American forces at Pearl Harbor, thus beginning U.S. involvement in World War II. February 19, 1942, however, holds significance for far fewer people. It was on that date that President Franklin Roosevelt issued Executive Order 9066, empowering the Secretary of War and his military commanders to exclude groups of people from militarily sensitive areas on the west coast of the United States. While no ethnic group was specifically mentioned, the target was unmistakable. Within months, 120,000 Japanese Americans, American citizens and resident aliens of Japanese ancestry alike, were forced first to temporary Assembly Centers and then to one of ten permanent Relocation Centers in the interior of the United States.

Mrs. Henderson's students did not know they were writing for the historical record. They were told the essays were a class assignment for which they would receive a grade. The students were asked "to put down on paper that recollection which remained clearest and strongest in their thoughts of the evacuation and relocation period." The excerpts contained in this chapter convey a young person's perspective of one of the most traumatic periods in U.S. history.

Long-held racial prejudice and hatred against Japanese Americans reached a fever pitch during the immediate aftermath of Pearl Harbor. They were beaten and spat on, were refused service at restaurants and stores, and were shunned by former friends and colleagues. Japanese American children worried over the reception they would receive in school. "I went to school feeling like that I would get picked on. When I entered the school my school mates were very nice to me. Some of the boys gave me a dirty look and said bad things about me. I did not feel too bad because I knew that I was an American citizen and I would always be. This always gave me courage after that."

Fearing a possible Japanese invasion of the west coast and potential acts of sabotage by resident Japanese Americans, the government asked Japanese Americans to voluntarily move outside the established military zones. This effort failed and on March 24, 1942 the Army issued the first of what would total 108 Civilian Exclusion Orders, directing Japanese Americans to prepare for evacuation. Businesses, farms, homes, and personal property had to be sold at a fraction of the original cost or left in the care of others. Evacuees were told they could bring only what they could carry. "Then came the big task of packing. We first started by packing the things which we were going to store. Then we sold some of our household furnitures, such as the peano, sofa, stove etc. We also sold our car."

The "Citizens of the Seventh Grade" spent their first four months of incarceration at Tanforan, one of sixteen Assembly Centers, a former racetrack hastily converted to house the Japanese Americans. Living conditions were primitive. "There were only three in our family so we had to have a horse stable for our apartment. It smelled a little for a while but after we gave it a airing it was alright."

The relocation process from Assembly Centers to permanent camps began in late summer and early fall of 1942. "One afternoon I saw on the bulletin board a note saying we were going to Utah. My brother arranged to go first so we had to get ready twice as fast. Every day after that we cleaned, we packed, made boxes, frames, and oh! so many things. I thought we never will be in time but we did. We got our luggage and we started to get on the train."

Topaz Relocation Center was the final destination for almost all the Japanese Americans imprisoned at Tanforan. "We all got in some buses and traveled along. . . . Some barracks came in sight. . . . We then heard some music which was off tune a bit and learned it was played by the welcome band. . . . As I stepped on the ground the dust came up in my face. . . . This was Topaz!"

The residential area for evacuees consisted of thirty-four blocks, each containing twelve barracks designed to house 250–300 persons. The six rooms in each of the barracks averaged about 18 by 22 feet and housed a family of four or the same number of unrelated individuals. The newly arrived residents received few furnishings. "Standard equipment for living included a cot, matress, and blankets."

Though temperatures at Topaz ranged from an excruciatingly hot 106 degrees in the summer to a bone-chilling 30 degrees below zero in the winter, it was the ever-present wind and resulting dust that proved most irritating. "Our houses get full of sand and all our clothes get sand all over and we have to clean all our thing it takes us practically all night. And when we go to school you get sand in your eyes and in your mouth and can't even see across the street."

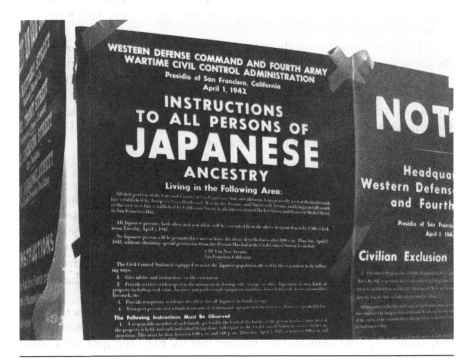

FIGURE 11.1   Exclusion Order posted at First and Front Streets directing removal of persons of Japanese ancestry from the San Francisco area, April 11, 1942. (ARC Identifier 536017, Variant Control Number NWDNS-210-G-A39, National Archives and Records Administration, College Park, MD)

For three years, Topaz Relocation Center housed approximately 8,000 Japanese Americans, the majority of whom were citizens of the United States. During those years 144 residents died, over one thousand graduated from Topaz High School, and fifteen young Japanese American men died in service to their country while serving in the Armed Forces. They died while their parents were confined behind a barbed wire fence patrolled by armed Military police.

&> Japanese American Internment Camp Essays cQ

PRE-EVACUATION

The Day the War Started

. . . My father said it would be nice to go for a little ride around San Francisco. The front door opened and I saw my father coming out of the house. Just as he entered the car we heard the telephone ringing and my father ran and opened the door.

He didn't come out for about ten minutes or so and my mother went into the house to see what was keeping my father. My mother didn't return so I put on the radio and was listening . . . suddenly the music was out and there was a flash I was listening with all my might. He started to say something and said Japan has attacked Pearl Harbor. I ran into the house to tell my folks. My father said that was my uncle and told him the war has been declared between Japan and America. I couldn't go for the ride . . .

At School the Next Day

When I heard about the attack on pearl Harbor on Dec. 7, 1941 I was helping my aunt on the farm. I was scared and frighten that even afraid to sleep. Next morning I went to school to find all my friends might turn against me but they didn't. That morning we had to listen to president Roosevelt's speech. I felt cold and small because when he said the word (jap!) all the eyes seems to turn upon me. I felt like hidding under the chair. I hope never again to have to go through that experience. . . .

Well when we reached our school the boys and girls who were not Japanese called us name and some started at us but were glad of the teacher because they were very kind to us and the teacher told the boys and girls who called

Watanabe, W. (Ed.). *Citizens of the seventh grade: Excerpts from compositions written by seventh grade students of the Topaz Junior High School on their experiences during evacuation.* Historical Section of the Project Reports Division, War Relocation Authority, Central Utah Project, 1943. (L. Tom Perry Special Collections, Harold B. Lee Library, Brigham Young University) us name not to call us names but be friendly like other times when we use to play together and use to have lots of fun. When recess came the boys and girls were quiet but still they were staring at us and they started to giggle over nothing at all and some of the boys and girls start to laugh and start whispering so we felt very funny then. When the school was over we just ranned home because the boys and girls was talking about us.

At school the next day I found most of my friends treating me as if nothing had happened. I was glad of this because I know they were my friends no matter what happened. After the bell had rung every body went into their rooms. Then we went into the auditorium and heard more about the terrible news. For the first time in my school years, I was really glad when school was let out for the day. I hurried home and getting my Japanese books went to the Japanese School with some of my girl friends. I waited for our teacher to come. When he didn't come at 4:00 o'clock we went home. From that day we never had any Japanese school.

I went to school feeling like that I would get picked on. When I entered the school my school mates were very nice to me. Some of the boys gave me a dirty look and said bad things about me. I did not feel too bad because I knew that I was an American citizen and I would always be. This always gave me courage after that.

The Next Few Months

When there came news of many Japanese taken by the Federal Bureau of Investigation, my father had my mother pack his clothes so that he would be ready to go if they came for him. That day was the dulles day I've ever seen. We all sat by the fire stove and just sat there. Every time we heard a car we would just jump up. Each time we thought they had come for my father. And soon the days went by and nothing much was heard of it. It sure was a relief for every one in my family.

Then one Saturday morning there was a knock at the door. To my surprise there stood a policeman. I led him into the house, trembling a little. I soon forgot my fears for he joked with us and had lots of fun. He asked my father if he had any gun. Now my father had an old gun someone had given to him so he showed it to the policeman. The policeman told my father that if my brother was old enough, he could have it, but since he wasn't, this policeman decided to take it. My father didn't want the gun for he never used for anything so he let the policeman have it gladly. I thought he had come for my father and I was glad.

Very soon after the war started, we had curfews. This meant that all Japanese must be off the streets by a certain time. In our city the curfew was eight o'clock. They had this in the paper and notices posted on the posts. If we wanted to play we went into the house and played or played in our back yard.

Most of the time, we listened to mystery stories on the radio. That was after eight o'clock.

About three and a half months after the war started, all the store run by Japan born Japanese, otherwise Japanese people that were not citizens of the United States of America, were forced to close their stores.

We were one of them. One night a Jewish broker, came to look our stock over. The next morning at nine o'clock he came again, with two trucks, several men, his wife and daughter. They came to take out our stock. They worked for three days and they got our store all emptied out.

EVACUATION

Preparation for Departure; Departure

It just didn't seem true! Moving from the place I was born, raised and half-educated. Moving from friends, not just ordinary friends, but life-long, dear friends. This also meant moving from the city we loved and everything about and around it. All of these things added up to losing something of very great importance which we dreaded to lose. We tried to grasp the meaning of it. Some people said, "Just a rumor." Some said, "Indeed it's true." But way deep in our hearts we knew it was no rumor, it was no matter that should be considered lightly, that it was something very important that would leave an impression for the rest of our lives. Although I was just a child I knew and could sense the terror of evacuation in my mother and father's eyes. It was worse enough to go but when we found out that we were the first contingent, that was quite depressing news. Our friends and relatives all gathered to see us off and when they whispered words of encouragement we realized there and then this was one means of showing our patriotism to our country.

Then came the big task of packing. We first started by packing the things which we were going to store. Then we sold some of our household furnitures, such as the peano, sofa, stove etc. We also sold our car.

After we stored our beds we slept on the floor, and cooked on a gas stove . . .

A girl named Mabel, who lived next door to the house that was next door to our house, was my best friend. We thought that since we lived so near to each other, we'll probably go to the same camp. But since her grandfather was a doctor, they were going to Turlock.

That disappointed me very much, to think that I had to separate with my best friend. Why! We were best friends since we were both in the first grade.

Knowing that we won't be seeing each other for long, we started to play with each other ever more than we did before . . .

One day Mabel and I decided to go to a movie together for the last time. After the show we went to the five and ten cent store.

When we went home we got the news that we were to evacuate to Tanforan.

Before we went my sister and I went into every room of our house and the garden and waved them goodbye.

FIGURE 11.2   Japanese Americans preparing to evacuate the West Coast, April 1942. (Library of Congress, Prints & Photographs Division, LC-USF34-072299-D)

8 o'clock found us waiting in the J.A.C.L. for the bus to come. 15 minutes later we were on the back seat of the greyhound bus with crowds of people outside bidding us good-bye.

As the bus started to move, I caught a last glimpse of our pink house. How I wished then, that I could stay . . . I was not happy, nor were my parents. But my little sister and brothers were overjoyed since it was their first ride on a greyhound bus. They didn't know why they were moving, they just thought that they were moving to another place. My mother was not happy. She was smiling but I could tell by her face that she was thinking of the hardships ahead of her.

When we came near the City Hall almost everyone in the bus looked out to see it, because they knew that it'll be a long time before they will ever see it again.

The ride was a pleasant one. It continued for about half an hour.

I looked out of the window and saw rows of little houses. My mother said that the place that we're going to will be something like that.

Soon the bus started to slow down. We had reached the gate of Tanforan.

Tanforan

On April 28, 1942 I went to Tanforan and the day was miserable because it was raining so hard and we had to go in the slushy mud and puddles. This day was a long weary day and the rain was leaking from the roof of the barrack and the latrine was up on the grandstand.

Our bags trunk and suitcase was wet and the beds weren't fixted and my brother and I unpacked the things and put them in a row and some of the mattress were gone so we got about four mattress from the barrack that was across from ours.

When we came to Tanforan I was surprised to see barbed wire fence all over the camp and soldiers outside the camp. After getting off the bus, they showed us a room we were to stay. It was just a barrack with partitions.

For about a week it very hard to get used the place because the life is so much different from what we used to live. I was very much surprised to see so much Japanese people.

And even on the bus my brother he said he felt terrible. And when we got to Tanforan. We waited until some boys showed us where we were to live. And finally some boys came and started to lead us where we lived. But when we got half way my brother felt so sick that he would not walk any more. So my father took him to the hospital. When my mother and I got there I was very disappointed because it was just a old barn that a horse once slept in.

There were only three in our family so we had to have a horse stable for our apartment.

It smelled a little for a while but after we gave it a airing it was alright. My neighbors were on the left there were three men one was old and crippled but he was cranky too. On the right my neighbors had two apts. They had three children and a mother and father.

Our mess hall had two parts and it was connected in the middle where they cooked and the halls on both sides were used for the place where the people ate.

One of the section was called the Brown Derby.

But of course most of us didn't think so when they served pork and beans and stew so much.

Thinking that it was about time for supper we set off. The road was very muddy. On the way I saw many peoples, who had just came in. They were all dressed in their best. Many of them had no umbrellas and were soaking wet. Children and babies were crying. Men were all carrying heavy baggages, and the women had tears in their eyes, making their way through the mud. I thought it must be very discouraging for them, getting their good shoes muddy, mud getting splashed on their clothes, and then finding that they were to live in a horse stall where it still smelled.

The next morning I thought I was back home. When I heard the noise of the straw mattress I knew I was in Tanforan.

FIGURE 11.3   Barracks for family living quarters at Tanforan Assembly Center. The former horse stables were hastily converted to house the arriving Japanese Americans. (ARC Identifier 53760, Variant Control Number NWDNS-210-G-C324, National Archives and Records Administration, College Park, MD)

I worked in the Camouflage project, and made lots of friends. It was very interesting work. The nets were suspended by chains and rope. Some of the nets were laid on the ground. We wound burlap into the net. We worked with three seasons color of burlap: green for summer, three different shades of brown for Autumn, and three blues for winter.

The Sunday lunch menu I memerized it. Because we always had it on Sunday. We had two hotdogs, icecream, cookies and potato salad. We had to stand in a long line at every meal. And we had to bring our own dishes. We had so many people we had to have two shifts.

Everyday we went to school, then one day it happened that our camp had to move to Relocation Centers and they had to stop teaching schools because all the of the teachers had to move to other camps. Soon all of our friends that we made in school had to move to Relocation Centers, we went to see them off, every morning people went to Arkansas, Ghila, Jerome, Tula Lake, Utah, Poston, Pomona. Soon it was our time to go there wasn't much people to say goodbye to because everybody had left already but we had some people to say goodbye to. They played "Old Lang Syne" that morning and it was very very sad.

RELOCATION

Departure from Tanforan: The Train Trip

One afternoon I saw on the bulletin board a note saying we were going to Utah. My brother arranged to go first so we had to get ready twice as fast. Every day after that we cleaned, we packed, made boxes, frames, and oh! so many things. I thought we never will be in time but we did. We got our luggage and we started to get on the train.

The train was puling away from our camp when a shout was heard I look out and saw people on the roofs of the stables waving and shouting. I felt very excited that night and could not go to sleep until about 2 o'clock.

When I awoke I found myself in a sort of dream. I looked around and I remembered we were on the train towards Utah. I went to the wash room and saw so many people I thought I'd never get through. During the time I was gazing out many of the people of the other cars were going back and forth to the dining car. I grew so hungry I thought I'd die. Eating oranges all morning did not taste good. At about 12:00 we ate breakfast.

It was like that all day. I looked out most of the time and kept on eating oranges which I do not like very much.

At night the officers came and told us to pull down the shades but we arranged to have it up but with our lights off. We had quite a time opening our window and now when we were asleep it grew cold and the wind changed and we could not shut it. So we slept with 2 or 3 coats and some blanket in the morning we reached Delta and boy was I glad.

Topaz

We all got in some buses and traveled along. I saw some little mounds which looked like Indian teepees. They were only mounds of dirt.

Some barracks came in sight. We came closer and saw some people.

Most of the people were sort of dark.

We then heard some music which was off tune a bit and learned it was played by the welcome band.

We finally got off. As I stepped on the ground the dust came up in my face. This was Topaz!

We have never been to a place where there was a dust storm before in our lives and I think it is very terrible and sometimes we have it for four straight day. Our houses get full of sand and all our clothes get sand all over and we have to clean all our thing it takes us practically all night. And when we go to school you get sand in your eyes and in your mouth and can't even see across the street.

FIGURE 11.4 Looking down a main thoroughfare at the Topaz Relocation Center, October 18, 1942. (ARC Identifier 538677, Variant Control Number NWDNS-210-G-E12, National Archives and Records Administration, College Park, MD)

We have had about two dust storms since we came here. It is terrible. The dust gets in our hair and sometimes the wind picks up tiny pieces of rocks. They would come against our legs and it hurted very much. The dust also gets through the window and under the door.

Many times we did not have our bandanas so that the dust gathers in our hair. We would tease each other and say, "Gee! You're an old lady or grandma."

Every place we go we cannot escape the dust. Inside of our houses, in the laundry and latrine and even a little dust gets in our mess hall.

I do not like the rain either. I do not have any rain boots or clothes. The ground around here gets very muddy and very often there are mud puddles. In the night time it is very hard to see the ground and so we slip all over the mud.

The snow is one thing I like. I never really seen snow or played in it. We go out into the lot next to our block and have a snow fight. We go out there to fight among ourselves but after we get started the boys would come and join us. We didn't even invite them but they come in. Everytime they chase us around to the next block.

. . . Topaz looked so big and enormous to me. It almost made me feel like a ant. A moment later we found ourselves walking through alkali dust. You certainly can't keep your brown or black shoes their original color because everywhere you walk is in that kind of dust. Your face and shoes turn white, also the dust collects on the legs making it chapped.

Scorpians and horntoads were all over. The boys had fine time finding them.

Under the supervision of the Army Engineer Corps, barrack type buildings were put up for us. These are frame construction usually covered with tar paper, and lined with wallboard. Each building is divided into compartments.

Twelve barrack buildings are grouped into a block, a mess hall, a recreation hall, and a laundry room.

Standard equipment for living included a cot, matress, and blankets.

Feeding is done in mess halls, located in each block. Menus include both American and Japanese type food.

Medical care is provided without charge to us, and a hospital is included in the center.

My home for the duration will be in this center. Although there is no life here, I guess I must get to like it.

Hot hot it was when we came here. But how cold it became when winter was here. We had a stove not enough coal to burn to keep us warm. We burned coal only in the morning because we did not have enough but not only that but it was warm after the sun came out. If we had the ceiling up it would have been warmer but since it was not put up yet, so much how we burned the stove it took long to warm the room. Before the ceiling was up a bucket of water left over night would be frozen in the morning. Finally when the weather became colder the ceiling was out up and more coal was brought to our block.

On August 28 we reached Topaz and the exciting trip made me wonder who found this dersert and why they put us in a place like this but I heard it is a good state to live duration of this long war.

All my friends think it will last about two years more but I hope this war will end very soon so I can go back to San Francisco and get the education more better.

I do wish this war will end as soon so it is possible because I do not like war and I know that everybody do not like war. This war is a horrible crime and if this crime do not end this is going to be a terrible world.

I hope Japan and America will declare peace.

I sometimes wonder how the garden in our home in San Francisco is coming along. Whether the plants withered and died and weeds cover the garden or the house was torn down and the sign that says "Real Estate—call so and so on so and so street to buy this place" covers the front while among the weeds which cover the lot blooms roses and violets. I wonder which is better—dying from lack of care or blooming among the weeds every year. Maybe someone has moved into the house (although it isn't very likely because the house is sort of old) and tended the garden with care and planted a victory garden among the flowers—that would be splendid and I hope that will happen. It would be better than the other things I have mentioned.

In the Classroom

Chronological Thinking

- Construct a time line of the significant events in the evacuation and relocation of Japanese Americans during World War II.
- Examine and interpret a timeline of the principal events and legislation in the history of Japanese immigration to the United States.

Historical Comprehension

- Locate the sites of the ten Relocation Centers on a map. Develop a theory and collect supporting evidence on why the government selected these locations.
- Write a narrative of the evacuation process from the perspective of a young Japanese American internee.

Historical Analysis and Interpretation

- Theorize what incidents might bring about the internment of an ethnic minority in the United States today.
- Analyze the attitudes and values present in the United States in 1942 which made the internment of Japanese Americans possible.

Historical Research Capabilities

- Potential Topics:
  Japanese American internment and evacuation
  Executive Order 9066   War Relocation Authority
  Immigration from Japan

Historical Issues-Analysis and Decision-Making

- Analyze the reasons German and Italian Americans were not interned during World War II.
- Write a letter to President Franklin Roosevelt proposing possible alternatives to the internment of Japanese Americans.

12

World War II: The Letters of Mary Anna Martin

"Last Tuesday evening we heard an announcement over the radio that the WASP program would be closed Dec. 20. It was quite a shock for all of us. All this training without a chance to use it." Twenty-two-year-old Mary Anna Martin, class of 44-W-10, was among the last group of Women Airforce Service Pilots to receive their wings. In letters to her parents, Mary Anna describes the exhilaration, fear, honor, and pride of being a member of the nation's first women pilots of military planes.

Formed in 1942, the Women Airforce Service Pilot (WASP) program trained women to replace male pilots sent overseas for combat duty. WASPs ferried planes from factories to bases, towed targets shot at with live ammunition for ground-to-air and air-to-air gunnery practice, and tested new, old, and rebuilt planes. They flew every aircraft in the Army Air Force fleet, from the smallest of trainers to the largest long-range bombers. When the United States called, 25,000 young women stepped forward, 1,830 were accepted into the program, and 1,074 successfully completed training. Thirty-eight women pilots gave their lives for their country.

The composition of the WASP program was geographically varied ("The rest of us girls are from Missouri, Pittsburgh, S. Carolina, and Chicago"), but there was almost no racial diversity. Following the standards of the time, African American women were excluded from service in the WASP. There were, however, two Chinese American recruits.

Program training was conducted at Avenger Field in Sweetwater, Texas, and differed only slightly from instruction received by male pilots. Days began early and ended late at night. "[W]e were up at

6:00, cleaned up the bay, made our beds, dressed and were in formation for breakfast at 6:25. At seven were sitting in class. Ground school was over at 10:00. 10:15 we went to drill. Then we were free to read our mail from 11:45–12:00. We changed our clothes and reported for the flight line at 1:30. At 7:00 left the flight line and ate dinner at 7:30. After dinner we thought well, we can rest until morning, but the officer of the day announced 'There will be a meeting of all trainees at 21:00'. This is my day!!."

Mary Anna was patriotic and adventurous and, like most WASPs, loved to fly. "I suppose you are interested in my trip last week. It was truly the thrill of a lifetime. . . . The trip from Ft. Sumner to Pueblo was the most wonderful experience since I have started flying. It was through the mountains, and with the clouds and snow around the peaks it made quite a picture." Danger, however, was always present. "I heard that a girl from W-6 was killed this morning in an AT 6 because she jumped too close to the ground . . . she evidently tried to ride the ship in and decided too late to jump." "One of the girls in 44-W-9 crashed on the long 2,000 mile cross country . . . she was off-course and evidently lost."

WASPs served in a civilian capacity during the program's existence, as the promise of official military status was never realized. This meant that recruits paid for their own transportation to Avenger Field, as well as for room and board and their own uniforms. "Just got back from getting the rest of our uniforms. The stuff has cost me only $15. This is everything I believe." The families of the thirty-eight pilots who died in service paid to have their daughters' remains sent home.

Knowing that hers was the final WASP class did not dampen Mary Anna's excitement at graduation. "Well the big day is over and I'm really excited! Those wings are certainly beautiful. The graduation affair was really one for the books. Movietone cameramen have been on the field since Monday getting ready for it." General Hap Arnold, Commanding General of the Army Air Force, told the graduating class that, "You and more than 900 of your sisters have shown that you can fly wingtip to wingtip with your bothers. If ever there was any doubt in anyone's mind that women can become skillful pilots, the WASP have dispelled that doubt. I want to stress how valuable I believe the whole WASP program has been for the country. . . . We of the Army Air Force are proud of you, we will never forget our debt to you."

After the program was disbanded in 1944, WASPs and their supporters continued to fight for the veteran status that would entitle them to benefits under the G.I. bill, veteran's health care, and a military funeral. When President Jimmy Carter signed Public Law 95–202 in 1977, the Women Airforce Service Pilots were finally recognized as veterans of the United States Armed Forces.

Mary Anna Martin was born in Liberty, Indiana on January 24, 1922. A graduate of DePauw University, she declined a fellowship at the University of Michigan to join the WASPs in 1944. In 1946, she married Eugene Wyall and had five children. She continued to fly after the war, first as a ferry pilot and then as a flight instructor, and became the unofficial historian for the Women Airforce Service Pilots.

℘ *The Letters of Mary Anna Martin* ℘

May 26th 19:00

Dearest Mother and Dad:

Gee, what a long day this has been. We came out in 2 huge semi-trailer trucks with benches arranged in the trailer, and have spent the <u>entire</u> afternoon marching here and there and in lengthy lectures from the chief of staff, the primary training (flying) officer, the flight surgeon and the physical training teacher. So far, I'm thrilled beyond measure.

Got a glimpse of the flight line when we went down to the hangars to get our flying "zoot suits" (Army fatigues) and other flying equipment.

18:00

Just got back from getting the rest of our uniforms. The stuff has cost me only $15. This is everything I believe.

Betty Phillips met me at the hotel and has been over quite a few times today.

Taps—

℘℘

May 27

6:30

This letter will have to be in diary form. I start to write and we "fall out" for something or other or else someone comes in to talk shop.

Gee, this radio has been a lifesaver. The reception is wonderful out here.

The weather so far has been <u>cold</u> and <u>rainy</u>. We've been wearing all of our uniform, T-shirts, shirts and J-2 jackets (leather flying jacket). There's a Texas gal in my bay and she is really taking a ribbing about the weather down here.

The rest of us girls are from Missouri, Pittsburgh, S. Carolina, and Chicago. We all get along swell.

Mary Anna Martin "Marty" Wyall, Mss. 262, The Woman's Collection, Texas Woman's University.

The regulation khaki pants we wear are called "G.P's" because a long time ago the girls did not have a unified dress. General Arnold was coming down and when Jacqueline Cochran got wind of it she ordered the girls to wear khaki slacks. After they were all outfitted, the general was detained in Washington and never came; hence the Generals' Pants.

This morning we get our shots. Well it's about time for breakfast. I'll write again later.

Dad, that letter was wonderful. We had just gotten settled in our bays and the mail orderly made her 1st delivery.

We have pre-flight on Monday a.m. and will begin to fly Tuesday. Yippee!!!

13:30

Have just finished lunch and are waiting inspection at 2:30. The shots were terrific. They got us in both arms, however the reactions aren't so disastrous.

Got you're 2nd letter while we were standing in line at the hospital. I'm glad you're getting started June 11th. I'll be thinking about you then. Well, I must mail this letter.

Love,
Mary Anna

P.S. Needless to say—these days are really hectic.

℘℩

Sunday, May 28
19:30

Dearest Mother and Dad, Louise and Grandma and Berney Dean:

Well, I still love it! This seems like dreamland down here. The state of Texas is different, but I can't see why anybody wouldn't like it.

We had our first inspection yesterday by an Army officer. All the girls in the new class really out did themselves. We passed satisfactorily.

Today the girls from W-9 loaned the girls in my bay primary manuals, so we spent most of afternoon sun-bathing between thunderstorms and reading about flying the army way.

There is a wonderful spirit among the girls down here. All the girls try to be so friendly—almost to the point they outdo themselves. They have a lot of cute songs for the W.A.S.P. We just heard a serenade from Class 44-W-9. Our flight lieutenant is my bay-mate and a swell girl. We had originated a new song to sing in cadence as we march tomorrow . . .

Well, goodnite—taps in 5 min.

Love,
Mary Anna

ℰᏩᏓᏗℛ

Thursday, June 1, 1944

Dearest Mother, Dad, Louise, Grandma and Berney Dean:

Well I've certainly had a taste of Army life. It's really rugged. We hardly have time to see the inside of our bays—Even our evenings are full of meetings and lectures.

We go out on the flight line very day and I get more thrilled about flying each time. Today they closed the PT flying during my period, hence, I didn't get to fly. Mr. Bingham talked to us students (5) for about 1½ hrs. which was just as helpful as actually flying. The wind velocity gets very high down here, that's why we didn't fly today.

I eat sand here all the time, but that's 100% better than battling with hot weather and insects. (I even like the snakes down here).

The other day I saw my first black widow spider. There are quite a few around here . . .

You've never seen such whiz kids as we are in our bay. This morning we were up at 6:00, cleaned up the bay, made our beds, dressed and were in formation for breakfast at 6:25. At seven were sitting in class. Ground school was over at 10:00. 10:15 we went to drill. Then we were free to read our mail from 11:45–12:00. We changed our clothes and reported for the flight line at 1:30. At 7:00 left the flight line and ate dinner at 7:30. After dinner we thought well, we can rest until morning, but the officer of the day announced "There will be a meeting of all trainees at 21:00". This is my day!! For the life of me I can't see where I've had the chance to gain 5 lbs. (I weigh 118 now).

Maybe Saturday I'll have a chance to mail my laundry bag back home.

Goodnight and love,
Mary Anna

P.S. You should see my sun burn. My nose looks like a "freshly pecked beak" (my instructor's words).

These are the pictures we took Sunday.

Mary

ℰᏩᏓᏗℛ

Sunday eve
June 4

Dearest Folks,

. . . Yesterday I got to land for the first time. It was a scream! I didn't have the slightest idea where the ground was and bounced about 20 feet. Instead of re-

FIGURE 12.1   Mary Anna Martin in a BT-13 at Avenger Field, Sweetwater, Texas. (Texas Woman's University, Woman's Collection, MSS 250.6.112)

covering for me Mr. Bingham let me recover my own bounces. This is an idea what it looked like ∨∨∨∧ I'm learning though . . .

Wouldn't you know! I'm the first one in the last ½ of W-10 (Flight #2) that got a demerit. During Friday inspection we roll our beds—that is, take off all the bedding and roll the mattress to the head of the bed. Well they didn't like the way I had my laundry bag tied to the bed. Isn't that childish? But that's the army I guess! I only have 6 to go tho before I get restricted for a weekend . . .

They've just announced that we will have a movie tonite. Think I'll go.

Well, I'll be thinking of you tomorrow on your wedding anniversary. And Louise, your graduation isn't far off is it? Your watch picture looks like a mighty lovely one.

Must hurry now
Mary Anna

෨෬

Tuesday, June 13th

Dearest Folks,

Got a letter you and Mary Louise and Glenn today. Yesterday the officer's sets came along with Mother's letter. Thank you, everybody!! The sets are perfect! I would never have thought of that. I shall send them immediately.

W-10 is really getting into the spirit of Avenger. Tonight there was really a free for all trying to duck everyone who soloed PT's today. Saturday the 1st girl soloed and perhaps by the end of the week we will have all soloed. Three of my bay-mates swam with the fishes in the wishing well. I thought that this was my day, but the anticipation of it all ruined my chances. This was my first really bad day. I was certainly off the beam. I knew I had a chance to solo, so I tried too hard. However, tomorrow I'm going to fly with a different attitude.

This morning we had quite a lengthy lecture on techniques of using a parachute. One of the officers had been in a special school for parachute instructors and we are to get quite a lot of training in the future! However, no jumps will be involved. The ironic thing of all is that this evening at supper I heard that a girl from W-6 was killed this morning in an AT 6 because she jumped too close to the ground. The rumor has it that she evidently tried to ride the ship in and decided too late to jump. We were just told today that if there's any doubt at all that the ship is going to crash—Jump! Noble pilots are not always safe pilots.

We got our dog tag yesterday and I feel like a honest-to-goodness WASP now. On the tag it says "Mary A. Martin WASP" . . .

Well taps in a couple of minutes. Keep on writing—I love it!

Love,
Mary Anna

෨෬

Thursday, June 15

Dearest Dad:

Happy Dad's day! I've got some good news for you. I hope it will compensate for flowers or somepin. I <u>soloed</u> yesterday. It was a wonderful feeling and made Mr. Bingham quite happy. Today I soloed again which makes my total solo time 20 minutes and total dual time 9 hrs and 56 minutes. We have been really hep on flying this week. The instructors are all anxious to get his students soloed. Mr. Bingham's five were all soloed by today. It's a grand old feeling to be up there all alone.

The most thrilling thing just happened a few minutes ago. Three B-17's (Flying Fortresses) buzzed the field in formation and then peeled off to land one at a time. A jeep rushed out to the planes and took the pilots to the O.D. (Officer of the Day) office. By that time everyone had rushed to the flight line to get the deal. Guess why they came. To pick up the girls from W-5 for a dance tonight. The girls in the graduating class were guests of honor. Wouldn't that be wonderful to go to a dance about 100 miles away in a B-17. I hope that happens to W-10 around in December.

I'll let you in on a little military secret (supposedly). Miss Cochran was here this week. She ate in the dining room with W-10 this noon. She's very charming and makes you at home.

Dad—I hope you have a happy Dad's Day. I'll be thinking of you . . .

Love
Mary Anna

ဆၢ

Thursday, June 30th

Dearest Everybody,

Gee, this has been an exciting week. That accounts for some of the reasons I've not written all week. First I must tell you that I'm back on the beam again in flying. I passed my civilian recheck on Friday and passed my 20 hour Army check Monday morning. It really made me happy. Lieut. Nance (the one who rode with me flunked 4 out of the eight whom he graded.) Today I have over 30 hours (11 solo) and am starting on the acrobatic stage. That's about all we do from now on in P.T.'s. The more I do them the better I like acrobatics. At first it scared me silly to do a spin, but after doing some everyday for a couple of weeks I've lost my tenseness. I actually can count the turns now.

Tuesday, the 27th, was graduation here at the field. It was the most impressive thing I've witnessed. It was 100 times more thrilling than college graduations. A band from Barkeley played for us. The classes all sat in the center section of the gym. After we had all filed in the graduating class in their blue uniforms marched in and we stood to sing the Army Air Corps song. The commanding officer gave about a one-minute speech and the wings were presented to the W-5 girls. Then as a tradition each class sings an original farewell song to the graduates . . .

Did I tell that we were moved to different bays? There were so many vacancies left by the girls who have been eliminated or have resigned that I have new baymates. They aren't as much fun as my 1st mates though. There are only five of us now instead of 6. One cutie from Vermont was eliminated yesterday. If I can last thru January, then the chances of being washed out are considerably low. If they know you can fly Stearmen P.T.-17's the army way, then you can fly anything. Of course, there is one thing about us that isn't so good. If we get sick and lose an excessive amount of time, it isn't possible for us to wash back to the next class. We are the <u>last to enter here.</u> Isn't that awful? You can imagine what it will be like next December when we are the remaining ones. No one will be here to see us graduate. Tomorrow was the day for the new class to come but Gen. Arnold made the announcement Tuesday (as you must know) that no more WASP training classes would enter. Whew!—I'm glad I'm here! The officials have definitely assured us that we <u>will graduate.</u> This has become quite an exclusive program Only 1,019 WASPs in all after we receive our wings . . .

That's all I can think of (at present). Write me about your vacation plans.

Love,
Marty

℘℘

August 1, 1944

Dearest Folks,

Well, I'm officially a third of the way thru the course. It's a wonderful feeling to have primary behind me. But, oh, those AT-6's are really something to look forward to. I'll send you a jumbo postcard as soon as I start flying them . . .

Love,
Mary Anna

℘℘

August 7, 1944

Dearest Folks,

Well, I feel like a freshman again. We were pre-flighted on the AT-6 and it's really an airplane. Geez, what a procedure we had to go through to stop and start the thing. Just to give you an example of what we do before we are ready to leave the ground. Make a visual inspection of the plane, get in, check Form 1, pump the wobble pump and primer pump five or 6 times, turn the magneto switch on and the generator and battery switch; push and hold energizer—toggle switch until it gains enough speed, clear prop area and engage starter. As the propeller starts to move it may need primeing. When engine starts push propeller setting on the quadrant to full low pitch after the oil pressure has reached 50 lbs. Isn't that horrible? Wait until we get the thing in the air and have to fool with the retractable landing gears . . .

Goodnight and love,
Mary Anna

℘℘

August 15, 1944

Dearest Mother, Dad, Louise and Grandma,

. . . There were a lot of unhappy girls that had to stay in this week-end for such minor things as forgetting to wear hairnets, leaving their parachute in the ready room and not reading the revised post regulations within a certain length of time. None of <u>us</u> fortunately had to suffer. On the contrary I had a very delightful weekend. Met a very nice cadet from Stamford. Someone new and he'll be here longer than my other friends . . .

When I was in Abilene I bought the most darling chalk-strip grey suit. It has a form fitting jacket with ¾ length sleeves and six plaits in the jacket. Of course, if we are excepted by the Army it will be yours, Louise. Oh yes, Louise, I found the most darling hat in town Saturday. It's something I can't wear down here. Too dressy! But just the thing for that black crepe dress of mine. It's a skull cap with little mirror studs so big ( ) and a gorgeous black veil. I wanted it the minute I saw it, so I took it. If I send it home, will you promise not to wear it out completely until I get home, Louise? I would think it would be nice for school. (Providing you <u>don't loan it</u> to some glamour puss.) . . .

The ground school classes are quite interesting now. We have 3 hrs. a day. One class is primary navigation—learning to plot cross countries, understanding of flight instruments and how to use our computers. Another class is maintenance—we are divided in groups of four and go to the various hangars to help the maintenance men in the inspections and repairing of the planes. My favorite hangar is #4—where they repair all the accidents. Then 3rd period we have link trainer. We fly a toy airplane by just instruments above. It's harder than actual flying I think. But fun though.

> Well, goodnight and love,
> *Mary Anna*

ᏚᏬ

August 17, 1944

Dearest Everybody,

I just received 3 very wonderful letters this morning. One from Louise, Mother and Dad. It sounds like you haven't been able to get settled down yet.

Here are the pictures that I forgot yesterday.

This morning my instructor was shouting like mad (as usual) but today it affected me as being very funny. He's trying to get me to learn to do the procedures so they go bang! bang! bang! and they're done. Today I was doing something and I was flub-dubbing around trying to do things in proper order, when Mr. Lamb said, "Martin, your Grandmother was slow but, damit, she's

<u>older</u> than you are." Little does he know! Another one of his pet expressions is—"You work like a 7-day clock." We all like him though. He reminds me a lot of Mr. Bingham. (My 1st primary instructor) I think it hurts him to see a student do a sloppy job of flying, because he gets such a disgusted "Oh my Goodness!" when I mess some maneuver up. Oh well, I'll get it eventually, I suppose. Everyone does what I do, at first.

　Until I hear from you again.

　Love,
　Mary Anna

℘)℘

August 24, 1944

Dearest Folks,

I have lots of news to tell you in this letter (for a change). But first I must tell you I <u>soloed</u> the AT-6. It happened at 10:04 Saturday morning. It was a wonderful way to start the week-end. Made 3 bad landings, but I got it down and that's the important thing . . .

　Oh yes, this weekend they had the state meeting of the Ninety-nines in Sweetwater so I joined. Do you know what that is? Amelia Earhart was one of the people who backed it, and the 99's were the charter members—all veteran women fliers. The national president is Miss Sheehy—who is our recruiting officer and visits the field quite often. She was here this weekend. I was a prospective member so I went to the dinner Sat. nite and the breakfast Sunday morning. Saturday the speakers were very interesting—our own director of flying (Major Hubbard) talked, then a WASP graduate (Oct, 1943) talked about towing targets in a Maurader (B-26) and some of the funny incidents she had experienced. Then the last girl to talk was the most interesting. She was one of the 15 girls (Americans) that flew over to England in the ATA (Air Transport Auxiliary). She flew Spitfires, Hurricanes and many other English fighters in England for 2 years. She's now a trainee here at Avenger . . .

　Today was a bad day for everyone in our flight. I didn't get to solo on my 3rd supervised—couldn't make any landings good enough to suit him. I'm glad in a way because we had two slight accidents on the field. Both happened on take-off—one the tail wheel locked and the girl recovered from without doing any damage, but the other was a ground-loop. She scraped a wing and then the engine caught afire. However, tomorrow I'd better do better. I can't stand 2 pink slips in a row. All of Mr. Lamb's students were in a slump today . . .

　Well, I must run—

　Love,
　Mary Anna

ℰꙩℭℛ

September 12, 1944

Dearest Folks,

. . . I suppose you are anxious to hear about the San Antonio trip.

I certainly love that city. It's almost like Venice. There is a river running thru the city and they have landscaped it with flowers, grass and walks running along it. The buildings are so picturesque . . .

Oh yes, I must tell you about the cute navy cadet I met in S. Antonio. Three of us were walking into a building to meet a couple of the girls and 3 navy cadets came out and noticed our fifinella pins and stood and stared then said "Wasps!" We were so astonished at some one recognizing us that we stopped and asked them how they knew. It happened that they had met some trainees that very week who were in San Antonio for their pressure chamber tests. His name is Don Richley and reminds me quite a bit of Preston. A very

FIGURE 12.2 Four members of the United States Women's Airforce Service Pilots (WASPs) receive final instructions as they chart a cross-country course on the flight line of a U.S. airport. They will be flying the B-26 Marauder medium bomber pictured in the background. (ARC Identifier 535781, Variant Control Number NWDNS-208-N-20843, National Archives and Records Administration, College Park, MD)

nice boy and was a former football player. I just saw him Friday evening and his leave expired 6:00 p.m. Saturday . . .

Well, Bob Hope is interrupting my letter, so <u>so long.</u>

Goodnight and love,
Marty

P.S. only 15 more week-ends till X-mas!

℘)℘

October 8, 1944

Dearest Folks,

. . . Last Tuesday evening we heard an announcement over the radio that the WASP program would be closed Dec. 20. It was quite a shock for all of us. All this training without a chance to use it. Then Mrs. Deaton called a meeting for all WASPs and trainees on the field. She gave us the news officially. But then told us something that made us cheerful too. C.A.A. has verbally promised to give all graduate WASPs a <u>commercial</u> license. That means I can take anyone up for a ride and can charge them for it, and it also means I can work towards my instructor's rating which is pretty hard to get. We get to keep our uniforms after the 20th of Dec. Oh yes, our graduation date has been set although weather may make it later, but it's set for the 9th of December . . .

Love,
Mary Anna

℘)℘

October 17, 1944

Dearest Folks,

Whew! What a day. Never a dull moment at the O.D. office. I'm Officer of the Day today. We had a very tragic thing happen this morning. One of the girls in 44-W-9 crashed on the long 2,000 mile cross country. It hit some of the girls in her class pretty hard. It seems that we go along so long that accidents never enter our minds. The news of her death so shocked the entire field that our C.O, and one of the staff officers immediately flew over to Memphis, Tenn. to take care of the situation. And they are trying to keep it as secret as possible so that it will not get into the newspapers. We haven't the slightest idea what happened, except that she was off-course and was evidently lost. However, we have had a marvelous record when it comes to fatal accidents, in fact, it is very much higher than the cadet record. But don't you worry about me. I'll always get her down sunny-side-up somehow. I do think I've missed part of flying though if I don't have a forced landing or get lost . . .

Well, it's about time for me to duck out for evening mess, which is welcome.

Goodnight and love,
Mary Anna

ℰↃℭℛ

14, November 1944

Dearest Mother and Dad,

Well, at last a minute to write you a short note. In about thirty minutes we go to the flight-line for our second night of flying. Last night, I went on a short cross country from 8:00 to 10:00. The lights were beautiful, so early in the evening all the farmers were still up and we could see little lights lit up all over the country. About 100 miles east of us we saw a thunderstorm from the lightning it ejected. Tonight he says he is going to check me out. Personally, I don't see how that is humanly possible to solo me tonight. However, I never thought I could fly the AT-6 in 8 hours either. Down here they never ask you IF you can do it, rather they say "You've shown me you can do it, now go up and prove it to yourself." It certainly must take a men of faith to be instructors.

I suppose you are interested in my trip last week. It was truly the thrill of a lifetime. We started Wednesday morning about 10:00 and flew into Avenger about 1:00 Sunday afternoon. The whole trip took in eight states, and we flew over some beautiful spots. Our first stop was at Fort Sumner, N. Mexico for gas. It is a transition school with P-40's and 51's. We ate lunch at Pueblo, Colorado. The trip form Ft. Sumner to Pueblo was the most wonderful experience since I have started flying. It was through the mountains, and with the clouds and snow around the peaks it made quite a picture. I had to fly at about 12,000 feet most of the way to clear the tops enough to avoid the downdrafts. Some peaks on my left quite a distance were from 14,000 to 16,000 feet high. Pueblo AAF was a B-24 base.

The trip to Pueblo, Colo. to Garden City, Kans.. was uneventful except that several of us got playful and flew formation until the Army broke it up. We stayed all night at Garden City AAF. It is a basic flying school, and reminded me quite a lot of Coffeyville. They had no room for us anywhere except in the hospital, so we had a ward to ourselves. It was inconvenient for us however; we had to dress and undress without lights. No blinds, and cadets in the other wards had plastered themselves at the windows trying to get a peek at the WASPs . . .

Well, I must go . . .

Bye—All my love,
Mary Anna

P.S. It's now 02:00 a.m. Wed. morning and I have just soloed the "6" in night flying. It was a thriller and I can't say I wasn't scared the first time around. In fact, it never dawned on me that I hadn't turned on my landing lights until I was on the final approach about 20 feet off the ground. Landing without lights is something you <u>don't</u> do until you are reasonably sure you can land with them on. When I realized what I was doing it was too late to turn them on, so decided to fly it into the ground and then I would know where it was the 2nd time it bounced. I held my breath until it hit the ground and was quite surprised when it turned out to be one of the best wheel landings I had ever done in a "six". Luck isn't the word for it.

Tomorrow I'll go in a cross country and will probably be through with night flying about Thursday nite. We only get 10 hours and I have 4 now. Night flying is really fine when you get accustomed to it.

Well g'nite and love,
Mary Anna

ℰℭℛ

November 28, 1944

Dearest Mother and Dad,

What a rat-race. I hope you haven't been too worried about my not writing. My hours are so irregular that I spend my spare time sleeping or getting fitted for my uniforms. It's quite a job getting ready for the big event. And from all reports it's going the thrill of a life time. We're each getting our <u>wings</u> pinned on us individually by a very important person. I can't tell you who right now, but it's worth the whole 7 minutes put together. Our graduation date changes daily but it moves between the 7th and the 9th of next week . . .

I certainly wish one of you would come down. This graduation means more to me than any college degree could ever mean. It sounds like the whole Army is going to make something out of it too. I wish I could tell you now, but for obvious reasons they don't want it known who will be present. In fact, that's why our graduation date is so tentative . . .

Well, it's bedtime (bed-check was 2 hours ago but we ignored it).

All my love,
Mary Anna

ℰℭℛ

December 7, 1944

Dearest Folks,

Well the big day is over and I'm really excited! Those wings are certainly beautiful. The graduation affair was really one for the books. Movietone cameramen have been on the field since Monday getting ready for it.

FIGURE 12.3 Avenger Field, Sweetwater, Texas. WASPs march off stage at Avenger Field, following graduation ceremonies of last class. (Texas Woman's University, Woman's Collection, MSS 250.9.24)

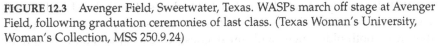

Last nite we were up til 1:00 recording while they were shooting us. Our class songs were especially beautiful so I hope they put them in. We had 4 generals here for the occasion as well as Miss Cochran. Gen. Arnold presented the wings and Miss Cochran gave us our diploma . . .

Well, goodnite from a very happy little duck in a big pond.

All my love,
Mary Anna

ৎৎৎ

December 10, 1944

Dearest Mother and Daddy,

. . . This last week has been quite eventful on top of the excitement of graduation. The movie cameramen took shots of us Friday morning until we were blue in the face. I certainly have a great deal more respect for Hedy Lamar than I used to have. They would keep having us repeat it over and over again until it was exactly as they wanted. Then in afternoon we really got in on a good deal. We ferryed some of our own planes down here to Concho Field at San Angelo. I flew a PT, then the C-47 and A-29, the planes which belonged to the photography outfit—came down to pick us up. I came back in the C-47 (it the Army converted airliner) . . .

Well I see my pen's about dry. I'll write again soon to give out with the private life of a W A S P.

Bye now, and all my love,
Mary Anna

℘◌

December 12, 1944
Tuesday eve

Dearest Folks,

. . . You know, some funny things have happened to me while I've been down here at San Angelo. On the first nite a G.I greenie gave Nancy and I a snappy salute and we were so dumb-founded that our hands remained in our pockets. Well, that ain't all. Today, I was walking along side the Officers Club and passed 2 officers talking. I stepped off the sidewalk to pass them and much to my embarrassment they came to attention and saluted me in a gallant manner. Well, I certainly was at a loss as to what to do—so I smiled and said "Thank you" in a very weak voice. I still don't get it because they weren't jestering—they were both older men (with mustaches). One a captain and the other a lieutenant. They cleared their throats and smiled faintly until I passed. Oh dear, I guess we must confuse everyone . . .

You would never guess where I'm writing this letter. I'm sitting on a trash can with a Rinso box for a desk in the "john" of the WAC barracks (after bed-check). The housing situation here at Goodfellow could not accommodate us so we had one choice of staying in town or bunking with the WAC. To say the least, we haven't been accepted with open arms, but on the other hand we're trying to make things as pleasant as possible . . .

Well, I should get some sack-time. Tomorrow we fly. See you next week for Christmas.

All my love,
Mary Anna

In the Classroom

Chronological Thinking

- Construct a time line of the significant events in the history of the Women Airforce Service Pilots.

- Examine how the service of women in the United States Armed Forces has changed since Mary Anna wrote her letters.

Historical Comprehension

- Conduct interviews with veterans of World War II to ascertain their memories of the WASPs and their thoughts on women in the military in general.
- Analyze the depiction of women in archival World War II posters.

Historical Analysis and Interpretation

- Write a newspaper article in opposition to the formation of the Women Airforce Service Pilots program.
- Write a letter from Mary Anna's perspective to her sister Louise describing WASP training.

Historical Research Capabilities

- Potential Topics:
  Women Airforce Service Pilots   Jacqueline Cochran
  General Henry "Hap" Arnold   Army Air Force
  Women in the United States Armed Forces

Historical Issues-Analysis and Decision-Making

- Identify and analyze the underlying factors that contributed to the termination of the WASP program.
- Analyze why it took over thirty years before the WASPs were officially recognized as veterans of the United States Armed Forces.

13

Civil Rights: Ernest Green and the Little Rock Nine

The 602 graduating high school seniors filed into Quigley Stadium on May 27, 1958 and took their seats. Parents struggled to locate sons and daughters among all those caps and gowns, but Lothaire S. Green had no difficulty finding her son, Ernest. The chairs on either side of where he sat were empty, for no other student would sit next to him. His was the only black face in that class of 602 students. "When they called my name, there were a few claps in the audience, probably from my family. Mostly there was this silence. It was eerie, quiet. But it was as if none of that mattered. I think the fact that it was so silent was indicative of the fact that I had done something. And really all nine of us had."

Ernest Green. Elizabeth Eckford. Jefferson Thomas. Terrence Roberts. Carlotta Walls. Minnijean Brown. Gloria Ray. Thelma Mothershed. Melba Pattillo. The individual names hold little significance for most people today, but the "Little Rock Nine," as they became known collectively, will be forever etched into America's memory. In May 1954, the United States Supreme Court ruled that segregation in public schools was unconstitutional. Three years later, the entire world watched as nine African American teenagers in Little Rock, Arkansas sought the right to an equal education.

The Little Rock School Board adopted a plan of gradual integration that would begin at the secondary level. "In the spring of '57, before we left school for the summer, each teacher gathered names of interested students. I put my name in, and that's where I left it. I don't think anybody really focused a great deal on it. If I got in, fine." Of the eighty students who initially expressed an interest, seventeen were selected based upon their grades and interviews with the Superintendent and his staff. Eight later decided to remain at all-black Horace Mann High School. The remaining nine African American students were scheduled to begin the 1957–58 school year at all-white Central High School.

Governor Orval Faubus, an ardent segregationist, ordered the Arkansas National Guard to surround Central High School preventing the nine students from entering on September 4, 1957. A second attempt was made on September 23. The students entered through a side door and were taken directly to the principal's office. The mob outside immediately became uncontrollable when it heard the students were in the building. Law enforcement personnel, fearing for the students' safety, led them through a rear door and returned them home. "I didn't hear any of the mob outside. When we were whisked out of school back to our homes, we sat there and watched it on TV. This is real, I thought. This is no day at the beach."

The school year finally began for the nine students on September 25, but it took the 101st Airborne Division to get them safely into Central High. "The next day we were picked up by the army at our individual houses . . . we got into a station wagon. It was a convoy. They had a jeep in front, a jeep behind, and armed soldiers in each of them. I think there were machine-gun mounts on the back of the jeeps . . . as we got out of the station wagon, a cordon of soldiers surrounded us. They marched, and we kind of strolled along, walking up the steps."

At first, conditions inside the school were rather tranquil, but the situation took a decided turn for the worse when the federal troops were removed. "[Y]ou were subjected to all kinds of taunts, someone attempting to trip you, pour ink on you, in some other way ruin your clothing, and at worst, someone physically attacking you. I never had ink thrown on me. I got hit with water guns. We got calls at all times of the night—people saying they were going to have acid in the water guns and they were going to squirt it in our faces."

Not all the other students at Central High School were opposed to the presence of the nine African Americans. "Initially there were some white kids who attempted to be friendly with us, but they were pressured. . . . If any of them were seen talking to us, they would get phone calls. They were called 'nigger lover.'" The nine students gathered strength and support both from each other and from the black community in Little Rock. "We each had different strengths and helped each other. I was probably the most stoic. . . . Our personalities tended to complement each other. We were nine different people, nine different approaches to solving problems. We were a good fit. . . . We also got a burst of energy from the black part of Little Rock, which really began to rally around us. . . . Everybody was saying very encouraging things.

While you were in there fighting those battles daily by yourself, it helped that other people thought very positively about what you were doing."

When Ernest Green walked across the stage and received his diploma on May 27, 1958, he became the first African American to graduate from Central High School. The struggle, however, was far from over. It wasn't until the fall of 1972, fourteen years after Ernest Green's graduation, that all grade levels in the Little Rock Public Schools were integrated.

Ernest Green went on to receive a B.S. in Social Science and Masters in Sociology from Michigan State University. He has received honorary doctorates from Michigan State University, Tougaloo College, and Central State University. He served as Assistant Secretary in the Department of Labor under President Jimmy Carter. He currently works for Lehman Brothers and lives in Washington, D.C. with his wife Phyllis and their three children.

&ropos; *Ernest Green* &roppos;

In the spring of 1957, the Little Rock school board finally agreed to desegregate grades ten through twelve. It was going to occur at Central High School [an all-white school].

We all knew Central. And in many cases the course books that we used were hand-me-downs from Central. You could tell because they had Central students' names in them. You didn't have to be a rocket scientist to figure out that the building, the course curriculum, the laboratory facilities, all of that was significantly different from what we had at Horace Mann, the black high school.

In Little Rock you never thought of yourself as being "Deep South." Deep South was going to Jackson, Mississippi, or Birmingham, Alabama. The year before we went to Central, both the city buses in Little Rock and the public libraries were integrated without any problems. The university had accepted some black students, and while it was difficult, they were surviving and doing their course work. So my expectations were that there would be words and taunts, but over a period of time that would blow over. I didn't think there'd be anything I couldn't handle.

And it seemed to me an opportunity to participate in something new. I knew it was going to be a change in Little Rock—I was smart enough to fig-

ure that out—but I didn't realize it was going to have impact beyond Little Rock.

In the spring of '57, before we left school for the summer, each teacher gathered names of interested students. I put my name in, and that's where I left it. I don't think anybody really focused a great deal on it. If I got in, fine. I talked with my mother about it. She said if I wanted to go and I was accepted, she would support me.

People like my mother and my grandfather, who was a postman and had attempted to vote in the Democratic primary, really are the backbone of the southern resistance. They didn't take a high public position, but in many ways expressed their indignation, their anger, and attempted to turn things around. My mother and my aunt were part of a lawsuit in the 1940s that filed for equal pay for black and white teachers.

We kids did it mainly because we didn't know any better. But our parents were willing to put their careers, their homes on the line. To me that says a lot.

Some time before school started, we learned there were limits on what black students were going to be allowed to do. You knew that you weren't going to play football, be in the band or the class play, go to the prom. I had

FIGURE 13.1 Elizabeth Eckford, one of the Little Rock Nine, attempts to enter Central High School on Septmeber 4, 1957. The angry mob threatens to lynch her. (United Press International) (Library of Congress, Prints & Photographs Division, LC-USZ62-126826)

been in the school band for five years from seventh grade through eleventh. Tenor sax. But this was as important enough breakthrough that all of those other activities, well, you could give them up.

I never expected it to be life-threatening, which it was initially. I didn't have any real sense of how dangerous it could have been until we got home. We were in this huge school, I didn't hear any of the mob outside. When we were whisked out of school back to our homes, we sat there and watched it on TV. This is real, I thought. This is no day at the beach.

The whole period has been cast in such a monochrome color that you don't get any of the tension and discussions going on in the black community. I'll never forget that afternoon. There were lots of black people who didn't think this was such a terrific idea. They saw it as disruptive, upsetting their personal lives. This neighbor of mine said, "You kids are crazy. The federal government is never going to support you. You're going to be out there by yourself and never get back into the school." Now that was real fear because I wanted to graduate that year.

President Eisenhower sent in the troops that night. There is an air force base about ten or fifteen miles from Little Rock. They were flying in a thousand paratroopers and support equipment. Lots of planes, probably a hundred or better, because they sent them in with all of their support material and jeeps and helicopters. I slept through all of that. Some people go hyper at crises. I usually get calm before and then I get hyper after I realize what I have done. So that night I didn't hear anything.

The next day we were picked up by the army at our individual houses and taken to Mrs. Bates's house, which was our gathering spot. From there we got into a station wagon. It was a convoy. They had a jeep in front, a jeep behind, and armed soldiers in each of them. I think there were machine-gun mounts on the back of the jeeps.

There were nine of us, and a station wagon was not very big. You had the driver, an officer in charge, and then us. We were all kind of squooshed in, riding along making jokes about it. There was no traffic, and no people were in front of Central. They had blocked off the school at least a half a block away. Nobody could enter without appropriate passes. I guess in army terms, they really had secured the area.

A helicopter was hovering overhead. You could see the news cameras across the street. And as we got out of the station wagon, a cordon of soldiers surrounded us. They marched, and we kind of strolled along, walking up the steps. Central is big, really built more like a college campus. The school is a couple of blocks long. A series of steps lead up to the front, which is very imposing. It was real drama going from the station wagon to the front door of the school. It probably took us four or five minutes just to walk up to the front of the steps.

Most people didn't believe Eisenhower would ever use that much force to get us back in school. I thought that that was important, but I had no idea

of the importance of it beyond my particular situation. Also, we had been out of school for three weeks, so all of us were getting a little itchy about getting further behind in our course work.

Every day the troops would bring us to the school. Initially we each had a paratrooper who would wait outside the classroom to escort us to the next class, so that we were never alone. All the troop personnel at the school were white, even though the army was integrated at that time. The black men were kept back at the air force base. I've run into both black and white men who were in that 101st Airborne Division assigned to Little Rock. Each of them that I met has said how proud he was to be assigned to that duty.

The officers had sidearms in the school. The first day or so they had rifles inside the school. When Governor Faubus said Arkansas was occupied, that was true. The first month with the troops and all of the media attention had been the point of high euphoria. In fact, conditions in the school were fairly tranquil. You had this great show of force. And also the most avid of the segregationists were boycotting classes at that point. When the segregationists realized that we weren't leaving, they started coming back. And when they came back, all hell started breaking loose. From around Thanksgiving until about March or April, it was really like having to fight hand-to-hand combat. It was trench warfare.

As they withdrew the troops from inside the corridors, you were subjected to all kinds of taunts, someone attempting to trip you, pour ink on you, in some other way ruin your clothing, and at worst, someone physically attacking you. I never had ink thrown on me. I got hit with water guns. We got calls at all times of the night—people saying they were going to have acid in the water guns and they were going to squirt it in our faces.

The biggest problems were in the halls and in physical education. In both places you had large numbers of students. The most difficult place for me was phys. ed., and that class was a requirement. The instructors just didn't want us there, and they didn't hide it a lot. When we were playing soccer or another activity, they didn't make any effort to pair you with students who were supportive. You got the feeling they deliberately put you with the most hostile kids.

When we'd come back to the locker room to shower, the students would always steam up the room and snap wet towels at us. It was a daily ritual. You just dreaded having to go to phys. ed.

You'd be crazy not to have fear. You kept fear in the back of your mind at all times., a fear that somebody was going to come over and physically harm you, and that nobody would come to your rescue. But we had to be nonviolent. Our nonviolence was an act of logic. We were nine students out of a couple of thousand.

The girls got it the most. There were six girls, three boys. Minniejean Brown, Elizabeth Eckford, Thelma Mothershed, Melba Pattillo, Gloria Ray, Carlotta Walls, Ernest Green, Terrance Roberts, Jefferson Thomas. With a

couple of the girls, people took their femininity as a weakness and attempted to take advantage of that. The segregationists, the Citizens Council, were trying to figure which one of us they could break.

Then they really took after Minnie. The incident with Minnie and the chili happened in the student line in the cafeteria. This was right before Christmas. We were all looking forward to the holidays because this was tough duty. We just wanted to get a break.

A small band of students had really raised the level of harassment with Minnie. I'll never forget this kid. He was like small dog snapping at Minnie with a steady stream of verbal abuse. He had figured out how many ways he could say "nigger." This kid just touched Minnie's last nerve. He was in front of her on the cafeteria line. I was behind her and I could see it coming. Before I could say "Minnie, don't do it. Forget him . . . " she had taken her bowl of chili and dumped it on his head. The chili just rolled down his face.

The cafeteria help in Central was black. They all broke into applause. The school board used the incident to suspend Minnie [but not the ones who harassed her], and then finally to expel her. And so coming back from Christmas, we were eight students. It was southern justice. They did what you'd expect them to do. In school, some students passed out little cards: "One down, eight to go."

Initially there were some white kids who attempted to be friendly with us, but they were pressured. The roughest period was after we came back for the second semester and the troops were withdrawn. The more avid racists really turned up the heat on other whites. If any of them were seen talking to us, they would get phone calls. They were called "nigger lover."

I remember doing a couple of radio programs with white kids interested in presenting a different point of view. Right after they appeared on the show, they received a great deal of hate mail and calls and pressure. I appreciated them trying to step forward, but we didn't have any sustained social relationship with them.

After the Christmas break, there was a great deal of pressure by the school authorities and business community to "normalize" conditions inside the school. There were still troops outside the school, but not in the halls and corridors. Well, of course, as the troops were withdrawn, the hostility increased. While the school authorities always talked about "normalizing" conditions, that year they just were never going to be normal.

I decided after the segregationists started coming back that I was going to make it through that year. Short of being shot, I could outlast anything they could give. I think it was a combination of the family support at home and the relationship that grew between the nine of us.

We each had different strengths and helped each other. I was probably the most stoic. As Terrance said, I only had to do it for one year. But I also thought that victory really was within our grasp. I thought we were probably

FIGURE 13.2 Ernest Green shows textbooks to young African American children after his first full day at Little Rock Central High School. (United Press International) (Library of Congress, Prints & Photographs Division, LC-USZ62-126834)

driving them crazier than they were driving us. This really was a war of nerves, endurance. If we kept all that in front of us, we could win. Our personalities tended to complement each other. We were nine different people, nine different approaches to solving problems. We were a good fit.

We also got a burst of energy from the black part of Little Rock, which really began to rally around us. They showed support in lots of different ways. One of the black sororities provided concert tickets for us. And the black leadership in Little Rock was with us. My minister and a number of others continually made public statements about how important and brave they thought we were. Everybody was saying very encouraging things. While you were in there fighting those battles daily by yourself, it helped that other people thought very positively about what you were doing.

Loads of letters came in. We heard from everywhere. The *New York Post* ran a series on us and described my interest in jazz. One fellow who was living in New York wrote me, and we carried on a correspondence for a number of years.

Over six hundred students were graduating, and there were honors and scholarships and all that. It's the irony of my class that no matter what any of the others did that night, they were all going to be overshadowed by one event—my graduation. I mean, they could be magna cum laude and have 59,000 scholarships, but that wasn't going to be the hook that people were going to remember.

We sat in these seats, and I had a space on both sides because nobody wanted to sit next to me. To get your diploma, you had to walk up a set of steps, across a platform, and back down. I had on this cap and gown. When they called my name, I was thinking, With all this attention, I don't want to trip. I just wanted to make sure I could stick my hand out to receive it and not fall on my face. No cosmic thoughts. Just very, very micro.

There was applause for every student. When they called my name, there were a few claps in the audience, probably from my family. Mostly there was this silence. It was eerie, quiet. But it was as if none of that mattered. I think the fact that it was so silent was indicative of the fact that I had done something. And really all nine of us had. Even though I was the one receiving the diploma, I couldn't have done it without the support of others.

Afterward I went to where my mother, my aunt, and my brother were. Dr. Martin Luther King was sitting with my family. I knew he was speaking in Pine Bluff at the black college, but I didn't know he was going to come up

FIGURE 13.3   Ernest Green and his mother are escorted to a taxi following graduation ceremonies at Central High School on May 27, 1958. (United Press International) (Library of Congress, Prints & Photographs Division, LC-USZ62-126830)

to Little Rock for my graduation. I had never met him before that. He had a plane to catch, so we just spent a brief period of time together.

At this point, I'm a high school graduate of sixteen. I've gotten a load off my shoulders, and I clearly was not interested in cosmic issues. I just wanted to go meet my friends. We were having a party over at the house and celebrating.

I had the broader view a few days before. I remember reading in the paper that my graduating was going to be a milestone. I thought to myself, This is great, but I want to do something else in life besides graduating from Little Rock Central High School. What do I do from here?

Little Rock, I think, became symbolic for a lot of things. It was one of the most televised of the desegregation cases. It was made for TV. It was good and evil. It was about as black and white as you could make life. You had nine kids who were innocent enough they couldn't have harmed a lot of people, and you had Governor Faubus playing the heavy. You had real drama.

One thing that I think is very important is this: while the nine of us may have been preselected, there really are nine, ten, thirty, forty, fifty kids in every community that could have done that. It wasn't that nine people fell out of the sky in Little Rock. We were all ordinary kids. You really do have the ability to do a lot more than either you've been told or you've been led to believe by your surroundings. If given the opportunity, you'd be surprised at how much you can do, how much you can achieve.

In the Classroom

Chronological Thinking

- Create a time line of the major events in the struggle for school integration.
- Place the events described in Ernest Green's narrative in temporal order.

Historical Comprehension

- Write a letter from Ernest Green's perspective describing his year at Central High School to a former schoolmate who remained at Horace Mann High School.
- Identify Ernest Green's motives for transferring to Central High School. Cite specific evidence from his narrative.

Historical Analysis and Interpretation

- Write an editorial for the Central High School newspaper from the perspective of a student who supported school segregation.
- Challenge the argument that segregated schools are not inherently unequal.

Historical Research Capabilities

- Potential Topics:
  school desegregation   Little Rock Nine
  Civil Rights   Governor Orval Faubus
  Brown v. Board of Education of Topeka, Kansas

Historical Issues-Analysis and Decision-Making

- Analyze the long-term results of the successful battle to integrate public schools.
- Identify examples of racism and bigotry that exist in today's society.